P9-CFO-243

forgiving
the DEAD MAN
WALKING

forgiving
the DEAD MAN
WALKING

Debbie Morris

with Gregg Lewis

ZondervanPublishingHouse
Grand Rapids, Michigan

A Division of HarperCollinsPublishers

Forgiving the Dead Man Walking
Copyright © 1998 by Debbie Morris

Requests for information should be addressed to:

🏛 ZondervanPublishingHouse
Grand Rapids, Michigan 49530

Library of Congress Cataloging-in-Publication Data

Morris, Debbie, 1964–.
    Forgiving the dead man walking : only one woman can tell the entire story /
Debbie Morris with Gregg Lewis.
        p.   cm.
        ISBN: 0-310-22265-6
        1. Morris, Debbie, 1964–   . 2. Victims of crimes—Louisiana—Madisonville—
Psychology. 3. Murder—Louisiana—Madisonville—Case studies. 4. Serial
murderers—Louisiana—Madisonville—Case studies. I. Lewis, Gregg, 1951–   . II.
Title.
HV6534.M224M67   1998
364.15'32'092—dc21
[b]   98-17616
                                                                                           CIP

This edition printed on acid-free paper and meets the American National Standards
Institute Z39.48 standard.

All Scripture quotations, unless otherwise indicated, are taken from the *Holy Bible:
New International Version®*. NIV®. Copyright © 1973, 1978, 1984 by International
Bible Society. Used by permission of Zondervan Publishing House. All rights
reserved.

All rights reserved. No part of this publication may be reproduced, stored in a
retrieval system, or transmitted in any form or by any means—electronic,
mechanical, photocopy, recording, or any other—except for brief quotations in
printed reviews, without the prior permission of the publisher.

Interior design by Sue Vandenberg Koppenol

Printed in the United States of America

98 99 00 01 02 03 04 05 /❖ DC/ 10 9 8 7 6 5 4 3 2

For Brad, Conner, and Courtney

CONTENTS

ACKNOWLEDGMENTS

Special thanks to

My husband, Brad, for being the most loving, patient, and generous man I know. Thank you for your tireless support and encouragement.

Mom, Dad, David, and Dionne for loving me unconditionally and trusting me to share a part of your lives in the pages that follow.

Judy and Ed for your faith in me in spite of your fear for me. Also, for your son, who happens to be the best husband in the world.

My friends at Zondervan Publishing House for your expertise and commitment to this book. Especially John Sloan, you're more than an editor. Your vision for this book made it possible. I thank you for your wisdom, your dedication, and your belief in me.

Gregg Lewis for too many things to name. I will always be grateful for your sensitivity, your gift of writing, your guidance. Thank you for helping me share some of the most painful and personal events of my life for the glory of God. Brad and I treasure your friendship.

Sister Helen Prejean for carrying the message of God's love and grace to Robert Lee Willie. Thank you for first encouraging me to write this book. My family and I are forever grateful for your friendship and prayers.

Ben Loeterman for your compassion and integrity. Your trustworthiness gave me the confidence to continue sharing my story.

The many people who served in the St. Tammany Parish Sheriff's Department and the St. Tammany Parish District Attorney's Office in 1980, particularly Mike

Varnado, Herb Alexander, and Bill Alford. Thank you for providing me with a sense of safety and significance, which helped me survive the initial days and months after my kidnapping. Herb and Bill, your help with recalling details and providing information has been invaluable.

Dr. Tim Alexander and Dr. Waylon Bailey for your pastoral care and spiritual guidance. You helped me stay focused on my priorities and my reason for writing this book.

Mark Brewster for surviving with me. Your strength and courage will forever inspire me. You will always have a special place in my heart.

CHAPTER ONE

Midnight at the Riverfront

I paid little attention as the glare of headlights briefly illuminated my boyfriend Mark's face and then swept on. I noticed the vehicle seemed to slow as it coasted past on the street right behind us. When it swung off the road and parked parallel to us a hundred feet or so up the riverfront, I noted only the outline of an old white pickup.

I saw nothing out of the ordinary. I felt no uneasiness, no fear.

Not in Madisonville, Louisiana.

Things had seemed even slower than usual in town that evening when we returned from nearby Covington after a typical pizza-and-a-movie date. We'd stopped at Badeaux's, Madisonville's one and only drive-in, for a midnight treat at about 11:30 or so. Passing on such house specialties as shrimp and catfish po' boys, we settled for milkshakes made with soft-serve ice cream and stirred individually on those old-fashioned machines. Mark ordered peanut butter; I got chocolate. Even though it was Friday night, there was no wait, no line at Badeaux's walk-up window.

Then we'd driven around the corner to sit by the river and enjoy our shakes. When we'd arrived, ours had been the only car parked on that entire stretch of riverfront between the tavern on the main highway at the river bridge and a little dockside seafood joint, a long block to the north.

Now there were two vehicles.

The quiet and surprising solitude seemed nice.

Century-old live-oak trees towered high above us, one on each side of Mark's '78 Thunderbird. Long, shroud-like clumps of Spanish moss hung from the limbs in the dark stillness overhead.

The car windows were rolled down. The muted strains of the rock group *Boston* filtered from the new Pioneer stereo—turned low so Mark and I could talk. Outside, early summer sounds of frogs and crickets drifted across the shadowy surface of the Tchefuncte River as it meandered the last mile of its winding course out of the swampy woodlands of southeastern Louisiana to its mouth on the north shore of Lake Pontchartrain.

Never one to let his car get cluttered, Mark had gotten out and thrown his milkshake cup in a nearby trash barrel as soon as he finished. He was behind the wheel again now, turned toward me. I sat sideways on the front bench seat, facing Mark, my legs tucked up under me, leaning back against the passenger-side door, still enjoying the last of my ice cream as we talked.

The white pickup had only been parked for a couple minutes when it backed out into the street.

I still sensed nothing out of the ordinary. Just the peaceful, familiar sights and sounds of home.

There could not have been many safer or more sheltered places in the world to grow up than Madisonville. With only eight hundred residents, it was such a close-knit community we regularly addressed many adults as "Auntie" or "Uncle" or "Granny So and So"—even when there was no blood relation we knew about.

There were, of course, some drawbacks to living in a small-town fishbowl where everyone knows everyone else's business. But Madisonville was the kind of place where my friends and I could walk into the corner grocery on the way home from school, pick up a bag of M&Ms and a Coke, and simply ask the checkout clerk to charge the afternoon snack to our families' accounts.

From the time as kids when we could ride a two-wheeler bicycle, we could go pretty much anywhere we wanted, provided we didn't cross the river bridge there on the riverfront where Highway 22 came into Madisonville, and we didn't go beyond Bayou Desire and the shipyard at the opposite end of town. Between those basic boundaries, wherever we might be riding or playing or visiting, our parents knew that one or two phone calls was usually all it ever took to check our whereabouts or beckon us home for supper.

No matter how much my own life had changed, no matter how many different houses we'd lived in, no matter how many stepparents, stepsiblings, and half siblings my brother, my sister, and I shared, our hometown never seemed to change. Indeed, for all of my life, the town of Madisonville, and the extended family who lived there, had provided me a greater sense of security and stability than my immediate family and my own parents had ever been able to manage.

Over Mark's shoulder I watched the white pickup roll slowly toward us again with its lights off before it swung in and parked parallel to the T-bird again. Maybe 25 feet away this time.

Though that seemed a little odd, I didn't say anything to Mark. Because I still felt no real uneasiness.

Not there on the riverfront.

While the main highway, State Route 22 between Mandeville and Pontchatoula, ran through the middle of town, the epicenter of life in Madisonville, the true heart and soul of the town, was the riverfront. It was here, just a stone's throw from where we were parked that night, that most of us learned to swim as kids in the slow, murky waters of the Tchefuncte River. It was here in the grassy patch of park between the street and the river that you could find many of the town's teenagers hanging out after dark on summer weekend evenings. All the traditional town celebrations—from Fourth of July parades when kids decorated their bikes in red, white, and blue to ride proudly in procession behind the fire trucks and police cars to local Mardi Gras parades filled with floats of costumed revelers—either started, ended, or at least passed along, the riverfront. When Santa arrived each Christmas, he always rode a boat down the Tchefuncte River, waving to townspeople gathered along these banks before he landed just below the bridge in front of the town hall and distributed gifts to all the children. When I was eleven years old I'd been selected with several other girls my age to dress as elves who rode right past this point with Santa on his boat and then helped him hand out the gifts.

Indeed many, if not most, of my happiest, most vivid childhood memories involved the riverfront. Everything fun, exciting, and good in Madisonville seemed to center around that very place Mark and I were stopped that night.

In the darkness, I could just make out two figures climbing out of the cab of the white pickup. If I didn't recognize the truck or the people in it, I figured Mark would. "You know these folks?" I asked him as two guys walked toward our car.

I'd been dating Mark Brewster for about eight months, since the fall of my sophomore year of high school. But since he was also from Madisonville, I'd known who he was and had known his family all my life. Which, given our age difference, was probably the only reason my grandfather ever let me go out with a twenty-year-old boy when I was just sixteen.

Mark had graduated from Covington High School the spring before I started there in tenth grade. While he had a brother my age, Mark and I hadn't gone to school together since he graduated from Madisonville Junior High School right next door to his parents' house. I'd seen him around town, of course, but the difference

in our ages meant we had two completely different cir-
cles of friends, as well as very different interests.

I remember the first night I ever really talked to him.
A group of my school friends bumped into Mark, his
brother, and some of their friends on the midway at the
St. Tammany Parish Fair. He and I spent some time
together that evening and seemed to enjoy each other's
company. Still, I had been completely surprised a day
or two later when he showed up at my grandparents'
house to ask me out for a real date.

Mark was just enough different from the fifteen- and
sixteen-year-old guys in my usual social circle at school
or at church to appeal to a small streak of rebellion in
me that prodded me to break out of, or at least stretch,
the usual mold of the responsible big sister and obe-
dient oldest child.

It wasn't as if I gave up my place in my familiar
social scene at church or at school. I was as active as
ever. But Mark didn't have much interest in the usual
high school scene of ball games and dances. In fact, he
used to tease me about that by calling me "Miss Prom
Queen."

Mark was one of those guys who marched to the
tune of a different drummer. And I enjoyed going with
him. While we had some typical pizza-and-a-movie dates
and attended a few rock concerts together in Baton
Rouge, he preferred spending time in the outdoors.

So once we got to know each other he'd borrow a
boat and take me along upriver to fish for catfish in
some nameless backwater of the Tchefuncte River. We'd
drive three-wheelers out into the woods for a picnic. Or
we'd water-ski up and down the riverfront behind one
of his friends' ski boats. On other occasions we'd go out
to the lakeshore when the tide was coming in and drop
crab nets from the old dock by the Coast Guard shed.
Some of our most memorable dates had been the times

we'd driven 24 miles across the Lake Pontchartrain Causeway to a lakeshore park in New Orleans where we'd fly kites Mark had created himself from tissue paper, scraps of cloth, and odd pieces of wood he'd found lying around in his house.

While I can't say I'd ever before cared much about fishing, crabbing, skiing, or even flying kites, I enjoyed doing all those things with Mark very much.

In some ways, Mark seemed a lot more mature than the guys my own age, in part maybe because he had already ventured out into the working world. He had a full-time job at the local shipyard where my dad, my grandpa, my uncles, and many of the men in town had worked for generations.

But in other ways, Mark seemed more socially awkward than other boys I knew. His outdoor interests in fishing and hunting required a lot of time on the water and in the woods alone. So he was still a little shy around people. Particularly girls.

I wouldn't characterize our relationship as super serious. I wasn't to the point of dreaming about wedding bells or baby carriages. But I certainly enjoyed Mark's company enough to be spending more and more time with him as the months went on.

And it may well have been some of the same spirit of rebelliousness which made me like him in the first place that had prompted me to stay out, sitting in Mark's car on the riverfront, so long past my usual 11 P.M. curfew. I knew my grandparents assumed I was spending the night with Mom out in the trailer parked in their side yard—the mobile home where my younger brother David and little sister Dionne and I officially lived with our mother when we weren't bunking inside Mimi and Poppie Pennington's house. I deliberately hadn't informed my grandparents that Mom had gone out on a date of her own that night. I told myself, *They'll feel obligated to stay up and wait for me, and I don't want to add to their worries.*

However, knowing Mom wouldn't be home yet and my grandfather wouldn't be waiting up, I'd really pushed my curfew limits on this particular Friday evening. Which had just become Saturday morning on the Madisonville riverfront.

My first inkling that anything was wrong came only after I'd asked Mark if he knew the two guys walking toward us. When he turned to look, he suddenly jumped and began furiously cranking up his window. Before he could get the window closed, a man's hand reached through and pointed a revolver right at Mark's head.

Suddenly another hand grabbed me around the neck from behind and a voice ordered, "Shut up! And don't do anything stupid."

The man on Mark's side yanked the driver's door open and forced Mark to slide into the middle of the front seat next to me. The other one opened the right rear door and climbed into the back seat directly behind me before leaning forward enough to put his arm around my neck again.

A voice from just behind my ear said, "We're escapees from Angola Prison. We've killed before and we'll kill again. Just do what we say and everything will be all right."

I knew if I'd scream I might awaken someone in the houses lining the other side of the street—maybe 75 feet away. But that thought flew right out of my mind when I felt the cool barrel of a sawed-off shotgun pressed against my left cheek.

CHAPTER TWO

"I've Got to Survive"

Looking back, I can't be sure how quickly the sudden shock wore off and the reality of our situation soaked in. But I remember the helpless, sick feeling in my stomach as my whole world went suddenly spinning wildly out of control. I remember the heart-pounding terror threatening to explode in my chest. I remember mind-clenching panic.

I was instantly frozen with fear. I couldn't even think, let alone react. All my life I'd heard the expression "scared stiff." That pretty much summed up the sensation I experienced in those next few minutes.

However, despite the all-consuming, almost over-whelming fear, what I remember even better was my immediate reaction to our captors: I was repulsed by them.

The first sensory impression I got from them there in the closed, dark interior of Mark's car wasn't what they looked like, but how they smelled. They reeked of sweat, body odor, unwashed clothing, bad breath, and stale beer, all mixed with an overpowering stench of what I eventually came to identify as Camel cigarette smoke.

What little I could tell about their appearance seemed to match their odor. They had long, stringy, greasy hair. The guy in the back seat sported a scraggly goatee. Their clothes were worse than grungy; the most fitting words I can think to describe them are "filthy" and "gross."

"Where are we going?" Mark wanted to know as our driver backed the T-Bird back out on the street.

"Shut up!"

"What are you going to do with us?"

"I said, 'Shut up!'" The gun at my head swung toward Mark. "Don't try anything stupid. We're gonna drive you out of town and let you go."

The driver also waved his revolver excitedly toward Mark as he drove. "All we want is your car and your money!" he assured us.

"Here! Take my money," Mark said, quickly reaching into his back pocket. His sudden movement prompted our skittish driver to swerve wildly as he jerked his gun around to point directly at Mark's face.

Mark slowly pulled out his wallet. "Take the money. Let her go right here. You don't need to take her outta town!"

I think that was about the time we passed by the darkened structure of St. Anselm Church.

My father's people were devout Catholics, as were my godparents, my aunt and uncle on my mother's side of the family. So it was there at St. Anselm that David, Dionne, and I were baptized as infants. It was there we attended catechism classes. It was there, one Christmas, when Father Adams invited the congregation to join in singing "Joy to the World," that three-year-old Dionne, recognizing the name of her favorite *Three Dog Night* hit, stood right up in the pew and enthusiastically began belting out the opening lyrics: "Jeremiah was a bullfrog . . ."

We all might have been more experienced church-goers if Mom had been a more committed Catholic when she and my father were married. She got up Sunday mornings and dressed us. But then she usually opted to stay home and clean house, trusting Dad to accompany us to mass. More often than not, instead of heading to church, he'd take us along with him to his favorite bar, the Riverview Lounge down on the riverfront. There Dad would spend an hour or two reading the Sunday paper, shooting the breeze with his buddies, and maybe downing a cold brew or two. Some days he'd proudly call me over to the bar and have me read something from the paper to impress his cronies. When we kids were finished performing, or watching TV, or grew tired of playing the tabletop bowling game over in one corner, we'd wander outside and throw sticks as far as we could out into the Tchefuncte River for the bar owner's black Labs to retrieve. And since Sunday morning cartoons and wet dogs always seemed to hold more appeal than traditional tunes and dry sermons, Dad's secret was always safe with us kids.

Despite his Sunday morning bar trips, and even after my parents' divorce when I was nine, Dad regularly expressed concern for our souls by complaining that Mom too often failed to get us up and dressed and out for mass on Sunday mornings "like he'd always tried to do."

When, as a junior high student, I'd started attending a Baptist church with friends, made my own personal commitment to Jesus, and decided to be baptized and officially become a member of the church, my father had been deeply offended. Not just that his oldest daughter had become a Protestant, but because "you've already been baptized a Catholic; that should be good enough for anyone."

Our driver took Mark's wallet and handed it to the man directly behind me. The sawed-off shotgun barrel wavered between us as he fumbled with his other hand to open the billfold.

On some almost subconscious level, I knew we shouldn't let them take us out of town. But I was still too scared to think of any plan to prevent it. Too scared to think, period.

I was aware enough to notice when we passed Coffee's Boiling Pot, the little hole-in-the-wall seafood restaurant about to open at the end of St. Ann Street, just three doors down from the trailer in my grandparents' yard. Looking up the block to the left in the darkness I saw the black outline of Poppie's giant pecan trees looming above the roof lines. I could see no lights in my grandparents' windows. Not that it mattered—I don't know that I'd ever felt so far from home.

"Thirty dollars!" came the angry voice from the back seat. "Oh, man! All he's got is thirty _____ dollars!"

"Take it!" Mark offered. "Take it all. Take the car! Just let us go! Let her go!"

"Shut up!" both captors ordered at once as their guns swung toward Mark.

"Here, Joe!" the voice behind me said, handing Mark's wallet back to the driver, who for some reason passed it back to Mark while trying to steer with his gun hand. That was about the time we drove by the darkened storefront of my Uncle Allen's grocery.

Mark's house was just one street over, bordering the Madisonville Junior High School playground. We were now just a few blocks from the edge of town.

Once we crossed Bayou Desire and drove by the shipyard, there would be nothing to the north but empty roads and pine forests for several miles. I wondered, *How far are they going to take us before they let us out? Probably far enough that they'll be long gone before we can walk back to town in the dark and summon help.*

Mark must have been wondering the same thing. "When are you going to let us go?" he asked.

"SHUT UP!" they told him again. I think that was the first time I consciously realized how tightly wound these guys were, how close to the edge they seemed. Instinctively, I knew the slightest provocation might set them off. I hoped Mark wouldn't try to say or do anything else.

During the last years of my parent's marriage I'd learned a thing or two about surviving tense or unpleasant situations. Whenever my father came home drunk or my parents got into some big, loud argument, the most effective strategy was always to retreat. If we were in a car or I was already in bed at night and couldn't physically get away from the angry sounds of conflict, I learned to pull back into myself, to withdraw and tune out the unpleasantness. And I learned never to say or do anything to call attention to my own presence.

Quiet withdrawal seemed like a pretty good strategy now as well.

We slowed slightly as we approached a gravel side road. "Keep going, Joe," the guy in back ordered.

"Okay, Willie." We sped up again.

I don't know what made me say it. I don't know how I managed to say anything. But I did. "Joe and Willie? Are those your names?"

Both men laughed awkwardly and the guy behind me said, " 'Course not! Them ain't our real names. We just call each other that. Ain't that right, Fred?"

"That's right, Jack!" They both laughed again and spent the next few miles calling each other Fred and Jack and then other names they were obviously making up.

I remember thinking, *Either these two guys think we're pretty stupid or they are none too bright themselves. Because they aren't fooling anyone with this little act.*

And I made a mental note. *Joe is the driver. Willie is the one in back. And Willie seems to be the one in charge.*

Willie was the one who said "Go left!" when the road forked just north of town. So instead of heading northeast toward Covington we angled northwest toward nothing on the Turnpike Highway. A few minutes after crossing a remote stretch of Interstate 12 we came to a black-topped intersection.

As the car slowed down, Mark said, "You could let us out here."

"I told you to shut up and I'm not gonna tell you again!" Willie shouted at him and jabbed him with his gun barrel.

"Which way?" Joe asked when we'd rolled to a stop. A right turn would have taken us east into Covington, right past my high school.

"Straight ahead," Willie told him and we continued on across Highway 190. "Slow down," he said a minute or so later at a smaller crossroad. "Turn here."

We turned right on Tantilla Ranch Road, headlights off now, and slowly coasted to a stop in the darkness some distance off the highway. "This is it," Willie said. "Let's get out!"

Joe removed the ignition keys, opened the driver side door, and got out. Willie prodded Mark with his gun and Mark slid across the seat away from me and out the open door. I didn't move.

"Stay put. Don't try anything funny!" Willie instructed me as he opened the back door behind me and got out. I was going nowhere. I was still so paralyzed with fear I couldn't have budged even if I'd felt there was a chance to run.

I heard a thud. Mark groaned when they hit him over the head with one of their guns. I couldn't see what all was happening, but I heard the trunk open and I felt the back end of the car sag a little as they lifted and shoved Mark's body into the trunk and closed it again.

Oh, no! Oh, no! That was the moment I realized, *They aren't going to let us go!*

I might have run right then. But I still couldn't make my muscles respond. Besides, there was no place to run.

Suddenly my door swung open. "Get out," Willie ordered.

When I still couldn't move, he grabbed my arm and jerked, "Come on!"

Somehow I managed to swing my legs out and stand. With the car doors open, the glow cast by the car's interior lights gave me my first real look at the one called "Willie." Scrawny, homely, not much taller than I was, maybe 5'6", he didn't appear too healthy. Rough looking to be sure, but he seemed more puny and pathetic than tough.

Except for the sawed-off shot gun and the look on his face. I didn't like the look on his face at all.

"Time to get in the back seat, Blondie," he grinned and motioned with the gun.

"Wha . . ."

"And take off your clothes!"

So that's what this is about.

I wanted to scream. I wanted to throw up. I wanted to die.

Instead I began to cry.

"No!" I pleaded. "Don't do this. What have I ever done to you. Please don . . ."

Willie stuck the shotgun barrel right in my face. "Get in the back seat! Now!"

I remember thinking to myself, *Be calm, Debbie. Be calm. Don't make him any angrier. There's nothing you can do about this.* So I did what I was told.

Willie got in the back with me. And when Joe climbed in behind the wheel Willie demanded, "Let's get outta here."

I didn't know if Mark had actually been unconscious. But when the car began to move, he started yelling and kicking at the top of the trunk. "SHUT UP!" Willie yelled, pounding on the back ledge of the car. I wasn't sure if Mark knew what was going on, but he kept up the commotion in the trunk as Joe turned the car around and pulled back onto the main highway heading north.

Willie returned his attention to me. "I told you to take your clothes off!"

"Please. No."

He raised the gun again. Again I began to do as I was told. The only illumination inside the car came from the faint radiance of the dashboard lights. That was just enough light for me to see Willie grin as he watched me remove my clothes. And it was more than enough to make me grateful for every bit of shadowy darkness in that back seat.

"Come on! Hurry up!" he said.

When Mark started shouting and pounding in the trunk once more, Willie told him to shut up again and laughed.

"Lay down," he ordered me.

I did what I was told. He carefully put his gun on the floor out of my reach. But his partner, Joe, reached over the back of the front seat with his right hand and held the pistol on me while Willie raped me.

I remember looking into that gun barrel and thinking, *As nervous as that driver is, as much as he's weaving the car and waving that around, all we have to do is hit one bump and that gun is going to go off.*

As strange as it may seem, I think the stark terror I felt at the prospect of being accidentally shot to death kept me from focusing so much on what was happening to me. It was like my mind wasn't really there in that back seat. I might not have been able to escape and get my body out, but my mind didn't have to stay. And it didn't.

I have a vague recollection of Willie's voice whispering in my ear, "If you make this good for me, Blondie, I'll let you go." And he said some other truly disgusting things as he raped me. But I tried to tune all that out by retreating into my mind, telling myself, *Just stay calm. You can find a way out of this.* As hard as it seems to believe now, it was at that very moment when I should have felt the most vulnerable, the most violated, that I began to feel as if I was taking back some control of the situation. I began to talk myself through the unspeakable ordeal. *You've got to survive. Fighting will only make things worse. There's nothing you can do. Accept it. Get it over with and then you can find a way out.* For some reason I was suddenly confident I could do that.

Willie sat up. It was over. I'd survived. Everything was quiet in the car and I realized I hadn't heard Mark making a ruckus in the trunk during the rape. *Is he okay back there? Or was it simply that he could hear what was happening and didn't want to make things any worse for me by further upsetting our kidnappers?*

"Can I put my clothes back on now?" I asked.

"Sure," Willie grinned. And he picked up his shotgun to keep me covered while I dressed.

We'd been driving north and then east toward the town of Folsom during the rape itself. Now we came to a major intersection where Willie told Joe to turn right —back south toward Covington and Madisonville. Toward home.

Covington had been home for the five years my mom had been married to her second husband. Wayne had four kids of his own, so we had a real houseful on the weekends. Maybe it wasn't quite the *Brady Bunch*, but those years were some of the happiest of my growing up—certainly some of the most normal and financially secure years my siblings and I ever had.

Wayne had a good job. He was a big Boy Scout leader, so we all got into scouting. We went to church together, camped a lot on weekends, and took memorable family vacations in Wayne's motor home.

I never did understand all the reasons Wayne and Mom started having problems. Maybe it was more effect than cause, but their first separation was about the time Mom developed a drinking problem of her own.

Mom and Wayne had broken up for good when I was going into the ninth grade. So I was fourteen when we moved back to Madisonville to live in the trailer in Poppie and Mimi's yard. But I'd lived in Covington long enough and made enough friends there, that when I was bused to Covington High School along with all my Madisonville friends at the beginning of our sophomore year, I already knew most of my classmates from both communities.

The closer we got to Covington and familiar territory, the higher my hopes rose.

Maybe they are going to let us go.

Since there had seemed to be some uncertainty at every crossroad we passed, I began to think, *These guys don't have a plan. They're just winging it. That could be good. Or it could be bad.*

I didn't know what to think. But at least I *was* thinking again. *We are heading back toward home. That's good, isn't it? But surely they can't just let us go now after what they've done. Not when we can identify them. Can they?*

I tried to hope—until we reached Interstate 12 and Willie said, "Turn here!" Joe wheeled onto the ramp marked East. Toward Slidell and the Mississippi border.

I knew then, *Something terrible is going to happen now.*

CHAPTER THREE

Gunshots and Promises

I tried to imagine, *If they're not going to let us go right away, what else could these guys be planning to do with us?* I didn't like any of the answers that came to mind.

Things seemed to be going from bad to worse in a hurry. *I've got to be able to do something. But what?* My body felt numb. Exhausted. Yet my mind raced furiously from one imagined scenario to another in search of some workable plan of escape.

"Where we headin'?" Joe wanted to know.

"Maybe we'll go to Florida," Willie told him.

"I don't know. Ya sure we want to go to Florida?"

"Yeah," Willie seemed to make up his mind at that very moment. "Florida will be great!"

"Don't think we got 'nuff gas to go clear to Florida," Joe protested. I couldn't see the gas gauge, but I knew it was almost a three hour drive across Mississippi and Alabama to the closest Florida border.

"There's a truck stop at Slidell. We can fill up there," Willie responded.

A few minutes later we turned off at the Slidell exit and pulled slowly into an all-night roadhouse with a handful of rigs parked off to the side, their drivers catching a few hours of sleep. Joe steered the T-bird to the pump farthest from the building and climbed out to fill the tank while Willie kept me covered with his shotgun and again threatened to kill me if I tried anything foolish.

I don't know what I'd have done if some trucker walked close by the car, but no one did. Joe topped off the tank, then went inside to pay for the gas and returned with four soft drinks. After driving far enough down the road to be away from the truck stop lights, we pulled onto the shoulder and they let Mark out of the trunk and gave us each one of the drinks.

Mark sat in the back with me. Willie got in front with his partner but turned so he could watch us and keep us covered with the shotgun.

I started to ask Mark if he was all right. "No talking!" Willie snapped.

Mark reached for my hand. "And no touching!" Willie told us.

I was relieved to see Mark and have him there with me again. But, at the same time, there was part of me that felt less safe. I worried that he'd try to do something. And that prospect scared me.

I'd already made up my mind I would endure whatever happened and just try to survive. But I realized that might be harder if Mark attempted to be a hero. As nervous as our captors were, there was no way we could communicate well enough to coordinate any kind of plan. It would be too risky. And not knowing what Mark was thinking actually made the situation feel more unpredictable and out of control than before.

To make matters worse, Joe and Willie seemed somehow edgier with Mark back in the car. Perhaps because Mark was bigger and physically stronger than either of them. Or maybe only because he was a guy and therefore seemed more of a threat. Whatever the reason, Willie maintained a much closer watch on the back seat than he had on me while Mark had been locked in the trunk.

Even so, one time when Willie glanced at the road ahead, Mark silently mouthed the words, "I'm sorry." I knew by the pained look on his face that he'd heard everything that had gone on when he'd been in the trunk.

I tried to give him a heartening smile. "Don't worry," I mouthed back. "I'm okay." Not only did I want to reassure him, but I wanted to keep him from getting upset and doing something crazy.

For the next few minutes we sat in silence, finding what comfort we could from each other's presence. We'd picked up Interstate 10 near Slidell and were heading east again toward the Mississippi border, with Alabama and Florida beyond.

I knew this stretch of road very well. If we were indeed heading toward Florida, we would have to go right through my father's hometown of Pascagoula. He lived there now with my new stepmother, her kids, and my little brother the two of them had together. This was a familiar route we traveled any time we went to Mississippi for a visit with Dad or our grandparents. In fact,

Dad was scheduled to come get Dionne and me early the next morning—(this morning now)—and take us back to Pascagoula for a long visit.

Because I knew what lay ahead, I began to visualize an escape scenario. If we stopped for one of the traffic lights going through Pascagoula, if there was anyone around, maybe I could throw open the door and make a break for it.

I knew the interstate ended in 50 miles or so at Gautier, Mississippi. That's where we would have to leave the limited-access highway and make a short jog over to pick up Highway 90 east through Pascagoula. *There might even be some kind of chance to escape along there. Just maybe. . . .*

We did exit the interstate at Gautier, just as I remembered. But before we reached the town itself, we pulled off on another dark stretch of shoulder. They made Mark get out of the back seat and into the trunk again.

Mark started to protest. But a quick jab of a gun barrel ended any argument.

Willie took the keys so he could drive, and they put me in the front seat between the two of them. So much for my plan to throw open a door and run if we stopped at a red light.

Maybe there would be another option. *They'll have to stop for gas again. Or food. Or to use the bathroom. If I just stay ready, I'll get my chance.*

Then I thought about Mark in the trunk. *If I did escape by myself, what would they do to him? Would I make his chances better or worse?* I didn't know the answer to that, and that really bothered me. I didn't want to do anything to further endanger Mark. *Maybe I should wait until they let him out. But maybe his only chance is for me to escape and get help.*

I couldn't seem to decide. Not that it mattered a whole lot as long as I sat wedged tight in the front seat between Joe and Willie.

A few minutes more passed before we reached Pascagoula. It was still the middle of the night, so the traffic lights through town were just blinking and we didn't ever have to stop.

We crossed the very street my father lived on, only a few blocks off Highway 90. But we never even slowed down. What hope I'd mustered as we'd approached Pascagoula faded quickly as we passed out of town and on eastward through the remainder of the night.

From Pascagoula it's only a thirty-minute ride across the Alabama border to Mobile. *Maybe there will be an opportunity there,* I remember thinking. *It will be daylight soon. More people out and about. More chances for escape.*

Neither Joe nor Willie bothered to keep their guns trained on me at this point. But they kept them in hand and ready. If I was going to have any chance of escape, I needed to get them to relax their guard. *Maybe if I get them talking.*

"So, where are we going?"

"Florida," said Willie, like there must have been something wrong with my hearing when they'd talked about it earlier.

"I know that," I said. "Where in Florida?"

They clearly hadn't thought that far ahead. "I don't know," Willie said. "Maybe Disney World. Or somewhere with a beach. You ever been to Florida?"

"Sure," I told him. "Lots of times."

"Where?"

"Lots of places." I named some.

We got back on the interstate right about the Alabama border, just before Mobile. We went through the city, into a tunnel, and were crossing a causeway over Mobile Bay when Mark started banging in the trunk again and yelling to let him out. The eastern sky was beginning to brighten. We stayed on the expressway past the exit to Gulf Shores and maybe another 10 miles.

Mark was really yelling by this time, "Let me out. I can't breathe. Let me out!" Willie shouted back at him to shut up, but it did no good. So Willie and Joe grew increasingly upset.

It was just after 6:30 A.M. when Willie pulled off at the Wilcox Road exit. The only thing there was a small convenience store with very little traffic that early on a Saturday morning. But it was light enough by this time that they couldn't risk stopping and opening the trunk where anyone might see. So Willie eased past the convenience store and turned west on what looked like a small service road that ran back alongside the expressway for a short distance before it curved away from the interstate. A little ways after we made the turn toward the south, Willie spotted a two-track dirt trail running back into the woods.

I wasn't ever sure if he'd been there before and knew where to look, or if he simply spotted the turnoff and figured it would serve his purpose. But the farther we drove back though the brush and into the trees, the more frightened I felt. We were out in the middle of nowhere, somewhere in Alabama. *No one will be looking for us within a hundred miles of here.*

Willie finally braked to a stop in a small clearing. "This is it," he announced. "End of the line. Everybody out!"

"Watch her!" Willie ordered. Joe stood by me, pistol out and ready, while Willie walked back and unlocked the trunk. Mark climbed out.

I didn't know if the stress and physical effects of a sleepless night had sent him into shock, or if exhaust fumes had been seeping up into the trunk. Mark seemed dazed and disoriented.

Willie kept him covered with his shotgun as he turned and grinned at me. "I'm gonna take yer boyfriend here out in the woods and let him go," he said. "Then we're gonna take you somewhere else and let you go. That way it'll take y'all longer to git together and us more time to git away." He seemed almost proud, as if he considered this an ingenious plan.

In a mocking, teasing tone he asked, "Anythin' y'all want to say to each other before he goes?"

Mark looked at me and said very softly, "I'm so sorry."

I tried to smile. "Everything's gonna be okay. Don't worry about me."

At that, Willie marched Mark off into the woods. I listened until the rustling sound of their footsteps faded completely away. Once they were gone, I decided to begin working on the one called Joe; I'd already realized he was the weak link of the pair. "What's going on?" I demanded. "What are you guys going to do with us?" He told me to be quiet and behave. But I kept right on. "I can't believe this is happening. We don't even know y'all. We never did anything to you. Why would you do this?" He wouldn't answer, but I kept right on pushing, trying to appeal to his conscience.

Ten, maybe fifteen minutes passed before I heard a single pair of footsteps coming back through the woods. It was Willie.

"C'mere, Joe," he said. "I wanna show you where I left him."

"What about her?" Joe motioned at me with the pistol.

"Lock her in the trunk."

"No, please!" I begged. I was terrified they wouldn't let me out. Plus, I knew once I was shut in that trunk there would be absolutely nothing I could do to escape.

What started as a feeling of sudden panic instantly turned to determined desperation. "I won't get in that trunk and you can't make me," I declared.

Willie completely lost his temper and screamed at me, waving his gun and saying, "Git in the trunk! NOW!"

I didn't move.

Willie swore. "I SAID NOW!"

I looked at Joe. "You gonna let me out?"

He nodded. "Sure. I'll let ya out."

"Promise? You gotta promise me you'll let me out."

"I promise I'll let ya out," he said.

"Okay," I agreed and walked slowly toward the back of the car. I climbed into the trunk and Willie closed the lid. Instantly it was night again, and I began to experience a major case of claustrophobia. It seemed like I could hear the deafening echo of my own heart pounding in terror. My mind resurrected a long-forgotten memory of an old *Dragnet* episode I'd seen as a kid. It had been about a young girl who had been kidnapped and then buried in a box. Now I was that girl and I felt like I too had been buried alive. Somehow I had to get out of that trunk!

A few minutes passed before I thought I heard something in the distance—the sounds of a struggle and then Mark's muffled, frightened voice. Too scared to listen, I put my hands over my ears and prayed, "Please, God, don't let anything bad happen to Mark!"

That's when I heard a gunshot. Horrified, I pulled my hands away from my ears and began to sob. Another shot sounded. Then silence.

A few seconds later, I heard someone running toward the car, crashing through the brush, crunching the dry, brittle grass with each footstep. I knew it was Willie and Joe, even before I heard their spine-chilling, maniacal laughter followed by a pair of animal-like screams that set me shivering and shaking all over.

Get ahold of yourself, I thought. *You've got to keep your wits about you if you're going to find a way out of this. It's all up to you now.*

I heard Joe right outside the car saying, "Give me the keys."

"That's okay," said Willie. "I'll drive now."

"I gotta let her out."

"We don't have time," Willie told him. "We gotta get out of here."

"I promised her, man. C'mon. Give me the keys. It'll only take a minute."

I heard the metallic sound of the key inserted into the lock and the trunk popped open to daylight again. "Hurry up! Let's go!" Willie snapped as I climbed out.

"What did you do with Mark!" I demanded to know.

"Us? Nothing!" Willie laughed wildly. "We didn't do nuthin'."

"I heard gun shots."

Willie held up his gun and replied, "Uh, that was me shootin' at some animal off in the brush."

My grandpa, my father, and my brother all hunted. I'd been around guns enough to realize the shots I'd heard hadn't come from any shotgun. "I know the shots came from that pistol." I pointed toward Joe's weapon.

"Okay, you're right," Willie admitted. "We fired a coupla shots in the air to scare yer boyfriend. You shoulda seen how he lit outta there." And he laughed again.

Okay. Maybe that's what happened. I really wanted to believe that.

"Now git in the car," Willie ordered, shoving me roughly into the back seat and scooting in after me. "Git us outta here, Joe!"

Within minutes we were back on I-10, headed east once more. And it was just after 7:37 Saturday morning. I made a mental note of the exact time because I'd made a determined decision during the time Willie was raping me: *I've got to notice and remember every detail so that when I get out of here and go to the police there will be no mistake about what happened. These guys will go to jail forever for what they've done!*

I was still trying to absorb what had happened to Mark and consider the potential implications when Willie pulled a big folding knife out of the front pocket of his tattered and dirt-stained blue jeans. He opened it up to reveal an ominous-looking blade, at least four inches long, and began to dig dirt out from under his fingernails. After he'd worked on a couple of fingers he looked over at me, held up the knife between us, grinned, and said, "I wonder what this would feel like sticking in that pretty skin of yours?"

Then he set about cleaning his nails again.

When he finished he looked at me again and said, "I reckon if I got ahold of you with this thing you wouldn't be so pretty now would you?" I didn't like what I saw in his eyes.

I didn't dare say a word. Without moving a muscle, I tried to shrink as far away from him as I could possibly get in that back seat.

Willie just watched me. And grinned.

CHAPTER FOUR

With Willie and Vaccaro

"Hey, Joe! We're almost to Florida." Willie's mood seemed lighter since we'd left Mark. We had only come ten miles or so since we got back on the expressway. But there was a sign announcing "Florida Welcome Station— One Mile Ahead." I remembered stopping there for free samples of orange juice when my family and I'd come this way before.

"Turn in here!" Willie instructed as we approached the off ramp to the visitors' center. Joe dutifully followed his command. There only seemed to be a handful of cars stopped at this hour of the morning. The lobby wasn't open yet. There was no one serving free juice.

"Let's go around back," Willie said, and we followed the signs for truck and bus parking. But when they saw a couple vehicles back there, he swore and ordered Joe to "Keep going!"

As disappointed as I was that we hadn't stopped and I hadn't gotten a chance to escape, by the time we'd pulled back on the highway again I was actually feeling encouraged. I felt certain Willie had been looking for a deserted spot where they could let me out. *That must mean they really are planning to let me go.*

"Ever been to Miami?" Willie asked me. "We could have a lot of fun if you'd go with us to Miami!"

"Do we really have to go to Florida?" Joe wanted to know.

"We're already *in* Florida. That there was the welcome station." Willie told his partner.

"I know that!" Joe replied. "But why're we goin' to Florida."

"To have fun!"

"But we ain't got no money," Joe protested.

I realized I had forty or fifty dollars cash with me. They had taken everything out of Mark's wallet, but they never even looked in my purse. I didn't say anything about my money, of course. I was more than content to wait and listen and see how their difference of opinion played out. A little disagreement as to their plans might just give me an edge I could use to get away.

"We'll just have to get some money," Willie said. "It's not like we haven't found money when we needed it before."

"But we don't know nobody in Florida," Joe argued.

"We'll make some friends. We already know Blondie here," Willie laughed.

Joe remained unconvinced. "But we ain't got no contacts. We don't even know where we can score some drugs."

Of course they'd need drugs. They'd probably been high when they first kidnapped us. *That would explain how wild and wired they'd been acting at the start.* But they hadn't done any drugs the whole time I'd been with them. *Maybe they're out. How long will it be before they need more? What are they going to do to get them? How is that going to affect my chances of escape?* I suddenly had a new set of questions I needed to consider.

Evidently Willie was thinking now too. Maybe Joe's mention of drugs changed his mind; something certainly did. "Slow down," he said as he studied the road ahead. "Up there! You can turn around there!"

We pulled across the median on one of those little dirt connectors with an "Authorized Vehicles Only" sign and completed a quick U-turn. Joe grinned, and we were all of a sudden retracing our trail back west again.

Such a complete reversal of course probably should have been a little disconcerting. After all, it was indicative of how unstable my two captors really were. However, I took heart in the fact that we were at least heading back toward familiar territory again.

"What are we doing now?" I asked to make sure.

Willie answered, "We're going home now. When we get closer, we'll let you go."

While I wanted to believe that, I'd just seen how quickly their plans could change. I knew I couldn't rely on their word. I had to stay ready. I would keep looking for some edge. I needed some kind of plan. Some way to get them off guard.

I'll try talking to them some more.

"We're going home, huh?" I asked.

"Yep," Joe replied, obviously pleased.

"That mean you guys are from around Madisonville?"

Willie looked at me a little warily. Like he wasn't sure how much he wanted to say. Or what I was hoping to find out.

I tried my best to make it seem like I was just being friendly. "I don't remember ever seeing you boys in Madisonville before."

Evidently, I'd managed to act disarming enough.

"I got me some kin around there," Willie admitted. "But I'm from over in Folsom. Joe here, he comes from Pearl River. You live right in Madisonville?"

I nodded. "Most of my life."

"How old're you, Blondie?"

I didn't see any reason not to tell the truth. "Sixteen."

Willie grinned. "Sweet sixteen?"

I didn't bother to respond.

"How old ya think I am?" Willie wanted to know.

"I don't know."

"Guess!"

When I wouldn't guess he told me, "Twenty-two. Born January 2, 1958." Then, as if he felt compelled to prove his integrity, he pulled out his wallet, extracted a folded piece of paper and handed it to me. "My parole papers from Angola!"

I opened it up to discover an official looking document complete with birth date, address, and full name: Robert Lee Willie.

"So, Willie is your last name?" It was a common surname in St. Tammany Parish.

"Yep," he said.

"What about him?" I nodded at his partner.

"His name is really Joe. Joseph Vaccaro. What's your name, Blondie?"

"Debbie. Debbie Cuevas," I told him.

"Got any brothers or sisters?" Robert Willie wanted to know.

So I told them about my family. That my parents were divorced and we lived with my grandparents. "My mom was a Pennington. There have been Penningtons in Madisonville more than a hundred years."

The more I talked, the more unreal the whole situation seemed. On the one hand, it felt so absurd to be making friendly small talk with these guys who had kidnapped and raped me. On the other hand, since neither one of these characters seemed bright enough to concentrate on too many things at once, I kept thinking that if we kept conversing as if nothing was wrong, they might gradually lower their guard. If they relaxed enough to put their weapons down, maybe, just maybe, I could grab one of the guns and fool them into thinking I knew how to use it.

But would I really be willing to shoot them if I had the opportunity? I didn't have to ponder that question for long. *If I can just get my hands on a gun, I'll use it! After what they've done to Mark and me, I'll have no qualms about killing either one of them,* I told myself. *No doubt about that.*

While neither of my captors set down their guns, my conversational strategy did seem to be having one positive effect. Where Robert Willie had been trying to intimidate me before, he suddenly seemed to turn friendly. Too friendly.

"We're headin' home now, Blondie. When we get there, we're gonna let you go!"

I wanted to believe that.

"Ya never know. Your boyfriend may've already hitched him a ride. He could beat you home."

I really wanted to believe that, too. *Maybe they're telling the truth. Maybe they had let Mark go. Maybe he really was okay.*

"You know," Robert Willie was saying. "I could be a better boyfriend for you than that other guy. If you was my gal, I sure would've stood up and fought for ya, at least. He didn't do nothin'!"

I couldn't help it; that made me really mad. "I guess it's easy being a big man when you've got a gun."

"Oooh, gonna git feisty on me are ya?" Robert Willie laughed. "She's a feisty one, Joe. She's purty and feisty, too. I like that in a chick."

As repulsed as I was by Robert Willie and this sudden turn in the tone of conversation, I didn't want to make him mad and threatening again. So I didn't risk any response to his insane notion that I would ever be his "chick." *Let him think that if he wants. Maybe it will help me.* But I just couldn't pretend to go along with him on this, so I simply quit talking for a while.

I was grateful Robert Willie didn't try to pursue our conversation. I was even more grateful when he announced he wanted to take a nap and instructed me to climb into the front seat where Joseph Vaccaro could drive and keep an eye on me. I figured once Willie was asleep I'd have only one to deal with and my odds of escape would look much better.

My previous judgment of Joseph Vaccaro's intelligence was confirmed as we drove through Mobile. When he asked me what one of the road signs had said, I suspected he couldn't even read. As pathetic as I thought that was, it gave me a little extra reason for hope.

I checked to make certain Robert Willie was still dozing behind me, then began working on Vaccaro once more. I kept my voice low, hoping it wouldn't carry into the back seat. The fact that we were approaching Pascagoula again, this time from the east, created an added sense of urgency for me.

"You know," I said softly, "since you're going to let me go anyway, you wouldn't have to drive me all the way back to Louisiana to do it. My father lives in this next town we're coming to. There's no reason you couldn't let me out here."

"I don't think so," Vaccaro said. "Willie said when we got back closer to home."

"But if you let me go now, you wouldn't have to watch me anymore. I don't know why you're doing this anyway. I can tell you don't want to hurt me. When we get into Pascagoula, you could just let me out and drive on without me. You wouldn't even have to wake Willie."

Vaccaro looked at me. "You're talkin' crazy now. I can't do that. Willie's my partner."

We were already at the outskirts of Pascagoula. I was feeling desperate. "He's not your partner. He's your boss. He's always ordering you around, always telling you what to do!"

"No, he's not!" That seemed to hit a nerve. But he was practically whispering, clearly afraid of waking Robert Willie and having our conversation overheard. He obviously didn't want his partner to think he couldn't handle things on his own.

"Well, it sure seems that way to me," I whispered back.

The light ahead turned red. It was the very street my father lived on. "You could stop right up here. We could both run off," I told him quickly. "I'd tell the police you helped me."

I probably shouldn't have mentioned the police. "Now you're really talkin' crazy," he told me. "No way I'm gonna be runnin' out on my partner."

We were coasting to a stop. I tensed my body to throw open the door and make a run for it. Silently I was praying some car would pull up alongside us at the light, and in my mind I started running through the steps I would have to go through to escape. First hit the power lock button to unlock the door. Then throw the door open, jump out, duck, and run. But Vaccaro still had the pistol. So I didn't know how I could hope to get away unless he agreed to let me go or showed some reluctance to shoot me.

"Please! You have to let me go!" I panicked and began to cry.

"Stop that! Stop that cryin' now!" Joseph Vaccaro demanded. "I can't stand it when a girl cries. Just stop it!"

"I can't help it," I sobbed. "My father lives right down this street. Let me go! Please!"

Vaccaro grew visibly upset. "You need to shut up with all that stuff now!"

"I can't!" I continued to sob uncontrollably.

"Shut up, girl. I said, shut up!"

At that Vaccaro lashed out with his right arm, and with his right fist still gripping the stock of his pistol, he punched me right in the chest with the back of his hand. Hard. The sudden blow knocked the air out of me and, at that very second, the light turned green again. Vaccaro began to accelerate and I was gasping for breath so hard there was no way to even think of jumping out and running.

The blow surprised me so much I quit crying. It also reminded me how helplessly unpredictable my situation truly was. No matter what clever strategy I planned, my captors were still very much in control. That realization, plus the fact that we were leaving Pascagoula again, triggered an almost overwhelming wave of despair.

What am I going to do, Lord? You have got to help me get away. I promise I'll never lie to my grandparents again.

It was a few minutes later, when we were almost to Gautier, before I managed to say another word. "We gotta stop," I said. "I need to go to the bathroom." Vaccaro looked at me suspiciously. But I was telling the truth, and I think he knew that. After all, it was midmorning now and I hadn't been to the bathroom since last night.

Vaccaro turned into a small gas station on the road running to Vancleave and Fontainbleau. He pulled the car around to the side, near the restroom doors.

Much to my disappointment, Vaccaro had woken Robert Willie up as we approached Gautier because he wasn't sure where we needed to turn north and he evidently didn't trust me to read the signs. So Willie warned me before we ever got out, "Don't even think about doing anything stupid or I'll kill you!" So much for any more sweet talk about wanting to be my boyfriend.

He and I got out. We walked to the door marked "Women." It was locked. Willie sent Joseph Vaccaro around front to ask the elderly woman working inside for the key. There was no key; she had to buzz us in. At the sound of the buzzer, I turned the knob and pushed the door open. Robert Willie started to follow me inside.

I stopped and turned. "No way!" I said angrily. "You're not coming in here with me!"

"Oh yes, I ..."

"Then I won't go!" I threatened.

He hesitated just an instant, so I pressed my argument. "Look!" I demanded, opening the door wide so he could see. "There's no window in here. This is the only door. I can't possibly escape. Where am I going to go?"

He looked. Then he turned and glanced nervously around to see if anyone might be watching us. He obviously didn't want to make any kind of scene, so giving in was quicker and simpler. "Okay," he conceded. "But I'll be right outside. And if you try anything, you're going to be very sorry." To underscore the threat, he twitched the gun he was holding down at his side.

After I went to the bathroom, I tried to clean up a little in the grubby sink. I felt filthy.

Robert Willie knocked impatiently on the door. "Hurry up! Let's go!"

I considered not unlocking the door, but I figured he'd get in easily enough. He had his gun after all; he could shoot the lock off. Or he might even go inside and simply force the old woman to open the door. *I don't want to get anybody else hurt. And there's no sense taking the risk of making him mad.* I really didn't have any doubt at this point that he could kill me.

So I opened the door and returned to the car. Willie drove now. And I was stuck in the front seat again, between the two of them.

Cruising westward along the interstate, Willie rifled through Mark's cassette collection looking for some music he wanted to listen to. He quickly settled on "Foghat! Live!" a southern rock band fairly popular in our part of the country at the time. He handed the tape to me and I inserted it into the stereo. The two of them really liked the cut titled "Slow Ride," so Joseph Vaccaro cranked up the sound. Then they wanted to rewind it and play the song again. And again.

I lost count of the number of times we listened to that one song. I know that, after a sleepless night, I felt as if the beat reverberating through the car was going to make my head explode. I finally reached over and turned the volume down to a saner level.

"Hey!" Robert Willie exclaimed. "I like that song. Turn it up!"

I didn't budge.

"Turn it up, Joe!" Vaccaro cranked it up full volume again.

I reached out and turned it down. "My head is splitting!"

"I don't care!" Willie repeated. "I like this song."

Vaccaro turned it up. I turned it down. When he turned it up again, I was so mad I shut the stereo completely off. Joseph Vaccaro tried to figure out what I'd done. But Mark's AM-FM stereo was a new model, one of the first where you had to depress the volume knob instead of turning it off and on. Joe couldn't figure it out.

"Let me try," Robert Willie demanded. He tried twisting the volume knob, looked in vain for a "power" button and then angrily pushed various combinations of buttons while he steered. No luck. "Okay, turn it back on," he told me after he finally gave up.

"My head is splitting. I need a little quiet."

"TURN IT ON!"

"I'll turn it on when I'm ready," I assured them. "In a little while."

I felt like laughing, but I didn't want to make them any angrier. They were already pretty mad.

So who cares? What are they going to do? Kill me? They're probably planning to do that anyway. They are still in complete control. Of everything but the stereo anyway.

I really might have laughed if I hadn't felt so much like crying.

CHAPTER FIVE

Chance to Escape

Every time I'd stood up to my captors and survived, I'd regained a little more boldness and emotional strength. After the bathroom incident, and our little confrontation over the car radio, I no longer worried they were going to blow my head off at any minute if I didn't do exactly as they said.

My conversational strategy also seemed to be paying off. Robert Willie seemed almost anxious to talk. Quite obviously, he was starting to like me. And as much as that thought still repulsed me, I hoped I'd be able to use this development to my advantage.

"Glad we ain't goin' to Florida," he said. "Maybe we could go out west instead. I ain't never been to California. You ever been to California?"

When I said I had, he seemed disappointed. "How 'bout Colorado? Ever been there?"

"No," I told him.

"Got me a friend just moved to Denver. I could take ya out there and show ya Colorado."

I was less than thrilled at that prospect. "I just want to go home," I told him.

"C'mon," he said. "You and me could run off together and pretend this never happened. I'd be good to ya. You're so beautiful! I'd change all my bad habits if I had a chick like you. I could really fall in love with you."

This was just too much. "How can you possibly expect me to forget this ever happened? You stole me!" (I deliberately avoided the word "kidnapped" because I didn't want to call any more attention than necessary to the seriousness of his crime—just in case he hadn't yet realized what serious legal trouble he was in.) "You do what you've done to me and you think I would run off to Colorado with you? That's crazy! I wouldn't go anywhere with you!"

"Are you saying you couldn't ever love me?" he wanted to know.

"How can you even ask?" *Doesn't he even realize what he's done?* I'd never in my life felt the kind of hatred I felt right then. I wanted to see Robert Willie rot in hell for what he had done to Mark and to me.

"Okay," he was saying. "Let's say you and me met somewhere under different circumstances? You might go out with me then, right?"

"No way!" I told him.

He acted genuinely surprised. "Why not?"

I could have listed any number of reasons, but I didn't want to antagonize him any more than I had already. "Well...," I stalled, trying to think of something to say that might not seem so much like a personal attack. "Uh ... because you obviously don't know how to treat women."

"That's not true!" He actually sounded offended.

"But look at what you've done to me!"

He brushed that point aside, went on to declare how much he loved women, and then began boasting about his sexual prowess. He evidently considered himself quite a ladies' man. "I know plenty 'bout how to treat women!" he concluded. "I've had me lots of 'em!"

"Obviously, none like me!" I said, making it clear I was unimpressed.

"That's true," he conceded. "Ain't never had no girl like you. You're so pure and innocent. What would a guy like me have to do to go out with a girl like you?"

"You couldn't," I told him.

"I could change," he insisted. "I really could. If I changed, what would I have to do to be able to go out with a girl like you?"

He clearly wasn't going to drop this, so I decided to answer his question. "Well, first you would have to ask me out."

"Okay," he nodded. "I could do that."

"And then, only if I was interested in going and said yes, then you'd have to come to my house and meet my grandpa."

"No way!" he responded. "I don't do that well with peoples' old men."

"Then you could never go out with me!"

Robert Willie shook his head in disbelief. "You tellin' me that you never go out with nobody 'less'n they talk to your granddaddy first?"

"That's the rule!"

"Okay, okay," he said. "Guess I could do that. Then what?"

"You'd have tell my grandpa where you were taking me and what exactly we were going to be doing."

He laughed at that. "I don't think he'd want to hear everything I'd be doing with you."

"See," I told him, "That's exactly what I meant when I said you don't know how to treat women. That's why I wouldn't have anything to do with you!"

"All right, all right," Robert Willie said. "You talkin' 'bout datin' in the old-fashioned sense. Okay. Where would I take a girl like you on a for-real date?"

"I don't know," I answered. "Maybe out to eat for dinner. To a movie. Or a concert."

"I could do that," he assured me. And then, as if to remind himself of the necessary steps, he reviewed what I'd said. "First, I'd have to ask you out and talk to your grandaddy. Then we'd go out on a real date. I s'pose I'd have to have you home by a certain curfew, huh?"

"Eleven," I told him. Even as I said it I thought, *If I'd been home at eleven last night, I wouldn't be here. This is the punishment I get for deceiving my grandparents! If I had done what I should have done—if I'd followed the rules—none of this would have happened.*

Clearly, Robert Willie was taking our highly hypothetical conversation very seriously. "Okay. I could do all that," he told me. "If that's what it would take for me to go out with you, I'd do it. 'Cause I could fall in love with you."

The further this went, the more uncomfortable I was with the conversation. So I reached out and turned the radio back on. I did it quickly enough that neither Robert Willie nor Joseph Vaccaro could tell exactly how I'd done it. Even so they seemed pleased to have music again.

"Turn it up, Joe," Willie directed his partner.

"Forget it, man!" Vaccaro replied. "She'll just turn it off again." So they left the volume at a reasonable level and I regained just a little bit more confidence.

It was after ten on Saturday morning. I'd been awake since Friday morning. Exhaustion had begun to set in. I knew I needed to be alert and sharp if I was ever going to escape, but I also knew I was going nowhere as long as I was stuck in the middle of the front seat of that car between two armed kidnappers. So I tried to get what rest I could by leaning my head back and thinking. As tired as I felt, as much as I wanted just to close my eyes, I told myself, *You have to stay alert. You have to keep your eyes open so you know exactly where you are and what's happening. You have to be able to tell the police everything.*

I thought too of my family. *Mimi and Poppie will be terribly upset. Mom will be hysterical. Dad will know by now that . . . DAD! He was driving over this morning to pick Dionne and me up! He might be on this stretch of road right now.* I sat back up straight to watch for my father's car.

Willie and Vaccaro were talking. "Know what we need?"

"Money!"

" 'Sides money. We need us some dope."

"Where we gonna get any dope out here?"

Robert Willie had an idea. "Let's find us a hitchhiker. Lots of hitchhikers carry a stash, so's they can catch rides with truckers and pay 'em off with dope."

I'd never heard that and didn't know whether or not it was true, but Willie and Vaccaro took it for gospel and began watching along the roadside far ahead in hopes of spotting a hitchhiker. Finally, along about Gulfport, they saw one.

"He looks like he'd have some drugs," Vaccaro decided as we drew nearer.

I had to agree. The man appeared to be wasted. Despite the fact that it was May 31 in Gulf Coast Mississippi, and the early summer heat and humidity had long since arrived, this guy was standing in the sun along the shoulder of an interstate entrance ramp, decked out in full army-surplus fatigues. Camouflage pants, olive-drab T-shirt, and a camouflage jacket, wearing a funny-looking hat and carrying a heavy backpack. A big man with long hair and a woolly beard that fell halfway down his chest, the guy looked downright scary to me. He was certainly not a person I would have ever picked up in a million years.

Once we passed him, Robert Willie wheeled over to the shoulder and stopped. As we waited for the guy to walk up to the car, Joseph Vaccaro tucked his gun hand out of sight under his other arm, so that the pistol's barrel rested right against my ribs. "Don't say nothin'," he warned.

"Don't even turn around to look at him!" Willie added, rolling down the window partway on the passenger side.

"Got any drugs on ya?" Joe asked when the hitch-hiker finally reached the car and bent over to look in the open window.

The guy glanced from Vaccaro, to me, to Robert Willie before he nodded. "Got a little hash."

"Get in, then," When Willie motioned toward the back seat, the guy opened the door and slid in. As we accelerated and pulled back out into traffic, I heard him rustling around in his pack. Without turning to see what he was doing, I assumed he was looking for the agreed-upon car fare. I was right.

A short while later he struck a match and then handed a foul-smelling pipe up to Joseph Vaccaro, who took one long drag and handed it past me to Robert Willie, who did the same before handing it back to our passenger. Evidently that was all the guy had, but Vaccaro and Willie seemed content again. As talkative as they'd been before, they were uncharacteristically quiet now.

The absurdity of the situation struck me funny. Here is a pathetic hitchhiker. Such a seedy, tough-looking character no one in his right mind would ever pick up. No telling how long he's been waiting for a ride. Finally, along comes a car that stops for him. He probably can't believe his good luck. And he doesn't have a clue that he's sharing his dope with a couple of armed kidnappers.

I couldn't help it. Maybe the strain was getting to me. Maybe I was simply giddy from exhaustion. I don't know. But I laughed right out loud.

I felt the gun pushed harder into my ribs. "What ya laughin' 'bout?" Vaccaro wanted to know.

Leaning over I whispered into his ear, "I probably ought to warn that poor guy y'all might not let him go."

Joseph Vaccaro thought that was funny, too. We both laughed.

"What's so funny?" Robert Willie snapped.

"Nothing," I told him, still laughing.

That upset Willie. "Tell me. What ya laughin' at?"

"None of your business," I told him. "You wouldn't appreciate it anyway!" That made me laugh even harder.

"What'd she say, Joe?" Willie was very angry now, probably thinking we were laughing at him. "What you two laughin' 'bout?"

"She's right," Vaccaro told him. "You wouldn't appreciate it!"

The fact that Joseph was simply mimicking me, plus the thought that he might never have used a word as big as "appreciate" in his entire life, made me laugh all the harder. I knew Robert Willie was furious, but I didn't care. He didn't do anything about it. And when I managed to quit laughing, I felt very pleased at the realization that I'd inadvertently driven another little wedge of resentment between my two captors. *Anything that divides them strengthens my position.*

The farther west we got, the more confident I grew. When we crossed the Mississippi-Louisiana border into St. Tammany Parish again, I felt as if I was practically home.

Willie and Vaccaro, on the other hand, acted increasingly nervous. Willie abruptly turned off at the Slidell exit, braked to a stop, and announced to the hitchhiker, "End of the line, buddy."

"Cops are bound to be lookin' fer this car by now," Willie explained after we'd driven away.

I'd been thinking the same thing for the last couple hours. It was another reason for my growing optimism. I imagined there would be APB's all over that part of the country. Certainly every policeman in St. Tammany and the surrounding parishes would be on the lookout for a black '78 T-bird with T-tops and red pinstripes. Such a distinctive car would be easy to spot.

"We're gonna need to stay off the main highways," Robert Willie decided. "But I know all the back roads between here and Folsom."

"You said you were going to let me go once we were back in Louisiana," I reminded him. "You could let me out right along here anywhere."

"I don't think so," Willie said. "There's a better place up between Folsom and Franklinton. We'll let you go when we get there. How does that sound, Joe. Know where I mean?" They both kind of laughed at that, and I didn't like the sound of it.

"What are we gonna do if a cop spots us before we get there?" Vaccaro wanted to know. "Won't we be better off without the girl?"

"You're right," Willie agreed. "But if any cop spots us, we can dump Blondie out and take off. While they're

checkin' on her, me and you'll have time to git away."
He turned to me. "If we see any cops, you better be
ready to move! We probably won't even come to a complete stop. You jes gonna have to leap out."

I nodded and thought, *Just slow down to forty and
I'll be glad to jump out of here.*

We stopped a little while later at some back-road
bar. Willie went in to get a couple beers for the two of
them and called someone in his family to ask if any
police had been around. "Cops ain't lookin' for us," he
told Joe when he got back in the car.

Of course, not, I thought. *There's probably nothing to
connect these two guys to Mark's and my disappearance.
What the police will be looking for is Mark's missing car.
And sooner or later, as long as we're driving it around,
someone is going to spot us.* My hopes were soaring.

I don't have any idea what back road we were on when
it happened.

Willie suddenly swore. "COPS!"

"Where?" Vaccaro jerked upright.

"Straight ahead. Comin' right at us, man."

"What we gonna do?"

Willie looked around. There was no place to pull off
or turn around.

The police car was still several hundred yards away.

This is it, I thought, trying to prepare myself for
whatever was about to happen. I was ready for anything—whether I had to duck a barrage of bullets or
dive out of a moving car. I was going to survive. I was
going to escape.

"It's a sheriff's car!" Vaccaro said.

"I just hope it's not Donald Sharp!" Willie said.

Both of them were swearing now. "What are we
gonna do?" Vaccaro kept asking.

"Shut up! I gotta think!" Willie told him. He wasn't slowing down to let me out.

As the police car drew closer, tensions rose and tightened and filled the car until I wondered that the windows didn't just pop out. I didn't dare say a word.

When the sheriff's car went past, I twisted around to look, expecting lights to flash and a siren sound to signal the wild chase to begin. But the police car kept right on going. It never even slowed down.

When it passed out of Robert Willie's sight in his rear view mirror, he whooped in joyous relief and Joseph Vaccaro joined in his laughter. "Ain't nobody lookin' for this car after all. We got nothin' to worry about!" They got suddenly brave and cocky again.

I kept looking back over my shoulder, waiting for the police car to reappear and give chase. When it didn't happen, all the hope I'd managed to muster over the past few hours sank right through the floorboard of that car. *If the sheriff's department in my home parish isn't looking for us, does anyone even know I'm gone?*

My spirits instantly plunged to a new low. There are no words I've ever been able to think of to describe the utter hopelessness and despair of that moment. I don't know that I could have been any more discouraged if I'd realized my situation was soon to get even worse.

CHAPTER SIX

"Kill Me Now!"

I knew I was now no more than a few miles from home. But I had never seen the deserted roads we took through the swampy backwoods of St. Tammany and Washington Parishes that Saturday afternoon. Evidently Joseph Vaccaro hadn't either.

He voiced the same question I had on my mind when he asked his partner, "Do you know where we are?"

Willie proudly claimed that this was all familiar territory. Not only had he grown up and lived all his life here, he said he'd learned "the lay-o'-the-land" driving a gravel truck up and down every dirt road for miles around. He knew exactly where we were going.

I finally regained enough emotional courage to speak up. "You promised you were going to let me go when we got back to Louisiana. When?"

"Soon," Willie responded. "Very soon. In fact, if you don't mind us leavin' ya out here in the sticks, we could let ya out right up here." He began to slow down. "What ya think, Joe? This look like a good spot?"

"I guess," Vaccaro agreed.

My heart pounded. I tensed up and leaned forward in anticipation. *Is it finally over? When I get out of the car, should I take off running into the woods and hide? Or should I simply start walking down the road?* The car slowed almost to a stop. I could feel the surge of adrenaline overtake the exhaustion. I was going to survive!

Then, just before the car coasted to a dead stop, Willie tromped on the gas and we went roaring on. As Willie laughed and Joseph Vaccaro joined in, I slumped back in the seat, feeling frustrated and furious.

"Don't worry," Willie assured me. "We'll have you home by five this afternoon." It was going on two already.

A little while later, on a different road, Robert Willie abruptly announced, "Up there looks like a good spot, Blondie. We'll let you out at that crossroad and you can find a ride back to Madisonville in no time."

He braked as we approached the intersection. Trying to get my bearings, I began wondering which road I needed to take if they indeed let me go. Then again, at the last second, Willie hit the gas and the two of them howled with laughter as the gravel flew and we raced on down the road.

I don't know how many times they pulled the same stunt. By the third or fourth time I refused to get my hopes up. Still, the torturous teasing took its toll. After a day and a half without sleep and no food since the night before, I could feel myself physically weakening to the point I wasn't sure I could manage to escape. And now, every time they pretended they would let me go and didn't, it left my psyche weaker as well, until it was anger more than hope that fueled what tiny shreds of strength and determination I had left.

At some point early that afternoon, Joseph Vaccaro said, "You sure are nicer than our last girlfriend."

When I didn't respond, he said to Robert Willie, "Ain't that right? Ain't she nicer'n our last girlfriend?"

"Yep," Willie grunted. "We got us a good'un this time."

Vaccaro smiled back at me. "I sure hope what happened to our last girlfriend don't happen to you."

"Why? What happened?"

"Oh! It was terrible!" his voice took on a strange, trance-like tone. "I don't know what happened but it was bad, real ..."

"Shut up!" Willie interrupted him. "Ain't no need to talk about that."

But it was as if Vaccaro never even heard him. " ... bad. Don't know what happened. Everythin' was fine and the next thing I knowed she was lying there without no clothes on ... and she was dead."

It was like he was having some kind of flashback and seeing it all in his mind. It was giving me the chills.

"She was all cut up and stabbed in the chest. It was terrible ..."

"I said SHUT UP!" Willie practically shouted. Vaccaro got quiet and very sad looking.

"I'm sorry," I said to Vaccaro. "That must have been terrible."

He didn't respond. The subject was dropped, and I tried not to think about what it had meant.

Between two and three o'clock we skirted Folsom and headed on north almost to Franklinton, when Robert Willie turned off Highway 25 onto yet another wash-board gravel roadway. I just caught a glimpse of the road sign, but I couldn't read it.

Within seconds, the road seemed too narrow. The shoulders disappeared and the thick green foliage of the forest seemed to press in from both sides and down from above. Of all the out-of-the-way places we'd driven that afternoon, this was decidedly the most remote and isolated spot I'd seen all day.

"Where are we going?" I asked anxiously. "Why did you bring me here?"

"Relax," Robert Willie told me. "We just want to check this out. We're looking for a place."

A place for what? I thought, but didn't ask. I was afraid I knew. *They aren't going to let me go. They are going to kill me and leave me out here in the middle of some alligator swamp where no one will ever find my body. There can't be another living soul for miles.*

But there was. We eased around a bend in the road and suddenly, in front of the car, walking toward us, were an elderly black man and a barefoot boy who must have been his grandson. The two of them, carrying cane poles and a coffee can of bait, looked like they knew where they were heading—probably some nearby stream or beaver pond that promised an afternoon of fun and a mess of fish for supper.

Robert Willie swore. "Oughta run over them niggers!" he threatened. But he didn't.

The old man raised his hand in greeting as we passed. I tried to look back in the rearview mirror, but the road twisted again and the two fisherman disappeared from my view.

I couldn't tell how much farther we traveled because we slowed to a tedious pace to negotiate the turns and steer clear of frequent, water-filled ruts in a bumpy roadbed that was in some stretches only a few inches higher than the swampy woods on either side. Eventually, the road forked and actually got narrower for a ways before we came to a small clearing with a pile of gravel and barely enough room to turn around. Willie wheeled the car around until it was headed out again. Then he stopped.

"What are we doing here?" I demanded to know.

"I don't know," Willie replied. "Maybe we'll all go swimmin'." He grinned at that. "You stay put! C'mon, Joe."

When they opened their car doors I could hear the sound of water running. There was a river, the Bogue Chitto I learned later, not far away. I noted the deep quiet of secluded woods and the occasional song from a swamp bird. But nothing else. No traffic noise. No other sounds of civilization. Nothing but the eerie sound of solitude.

I turned to see Willie and Vaccaro standing out of earshot behind the car. Their guns at their sides, they looked from me out to the road and back to me as they talked. While I couldn't be sure, I sensed they were concerned about the old man and the boy who'd seen us driving in.

After a couple of minutes Vaccaro wandered off out of sight in the woods and Robert Willie returned to the car. "Get in the back seat!" he ordered me. "And take off your clothes."

I had barely enough strength to protest, "Please, no!" Not nearly enough to resist.

By the time he finished raping me that second time, Vaccaro had returned. Willie threw my clothes at me and said, "You're finished! Now get dressed!"

I was a mess by this time. I felt so absolutely filthy I doubted that I would ever feel clean again. But I had nothing to clean up with except an old brown hand-kerchief I found on the floor of the back seat. So I used that. And when I finished getting dressed, I nonchalantly dropped the filthy little rag on the ground next to the car, hoping against hope that someone would find it and consider it a clue.

But Robert Willie spotted the handkerchief and exploded in rage. "What are you trying to do?"

I feigned innocence. "It was dirty!" I said, making a face, as if that explained everything.

"I don't care!" he snapped. "You don't throw anything out of this car! Do you hear me!?"

I nodded. But my response had evidently appeased him. He let the subject drop and we all got back in the front seat—with me in the middle again—and drove back out to the highway. I prayed, *Please God, you gotta help me get out of here alive.* And I wondered, *When is this all going to end?* I would have cried, but I wasn't going to give my captors the satisfaction of seeing me break down.

I watched for some sign of the two fishermen all the way back to the highway. But it was as if they'd completely disappeared.

We stopped a short while later at some little convenience store. Vaccaro went in and came back out with a six-pack of beer, a bag of chips, and a couple candy bars. While we drove around some more, they drank their beer and ate all the snack stuff without offering me a thing.

"We gotta find us some more drugs," Robert Willie decided. Vaccaro agreed. For the next several minutes, they discussed how they might go about doing that. Finally, one of them suggested, "Tommy Holden. He's always got a stash. We can get some from him. We jes' gotta find 'im."

Emboldened, or maybe just so desperate for drugs that they forgot about the possibility of getting caught, we headed back toward Covington, where we spent the remainder of the afternoon cruising around and around while Willie and Vaccaro looked for this Tommy Holden. For some reason, we spent a lot of time driving up and down River Road. I noticed a party going on in one of the yards along the way, and I remember being tempted to scream for help each time we drove by. But there was loud music at the party, and Mark's car stereo was blasting away, so I didn't think there was any hope I'd accomplish anything but make Robert Willie mad again.

I did hope that our repeated passings might catch the attention of someone at the party. *Surely if anyone saw me with these two guys in this car they'd suspect something was odd. At least they'll remember and be able to confirm my story of what really happened.*

But no one noticed.

It was after five o'clock, on Fitzsimmons Road somewhere between Lee Road and the Folsom Highway, when Vaccaro finally spotted the guy they were looking for. "There's Tommy." They flagged him down.

An ancient Chrysler New Yorker, painted green with orange stick-on racing stripes, pulled up beside us. "Nice wheels," Holden called through open windows. "Whose is it?" I noticed he slurred his words.

"Hers," Willie told him, nodding toward me. "But we gotta stash the car for a while. Can we get a ride with you?"

"Sure." Holden agreed and followed us back to a deserted stretch of River Road where we turned off and drove back along a power line right-of-way. "Just act like you're our girlfriend," Willie instructed me. "Make one false move and we'll kill you!" *At least they're not want-ing this Holden guy to know what's really going on. Maybe he would help me.*

We parked Mark's T-bird, concealed from the road behind a clump of bushes. Willie locked the car, put the keys in his pocket, and we climbed into the Chrysler which Tommy Holden had pulled up beside us.

Vaccaro got in front with Holden. Willie shoved me into the back seat ahead of him. "Where to?" asked Holden, showing no sign of having noticed two of his passengers were carrying guns. He turned to look at me and I figured out why. His eyes were bloodshot; he was clearly wasted.

If he was indeed a drug dealer, his car and his appearance labeled him "small-time." He looked like someone who'd associate with Willie and Vaccaro— unkempt hair, wearing a grubby black T-shirt, and sporting a variety of tattoos. I had no idea whether or not he'd have any qualms about being a willing accomplice to kidnapping or murder. I'd need time to discover how much, or if, I could depend on him. In the meantime, he seemed in no condition to be of immediate help.

Tommy Holden evidently wasn't even capable of driving. He got his car stuck in a muddy furrow just before we were going to pull back out on River Road. Robert Willie made me get out with him and Vaccaro to push. My shoes and jeans got caked with mud, which also splattered my hair and face.

No luck. Willie took me with him back to get Mark's car to push Holden out. Soon both cars were stuck.

It was about dusk when two guys drove by in a four-wheel-drive truck. Vaccaro got in the T-bird with me while Willie and Holden flagged them down. I realized this was the best chance for escape I'd had all day— maybe the last chance I would get—but I simply felt too scared and too tired to decide to make a break for it.

And since I wasn't allowed to get out of the car while they towed us from the mud, I didn't even have a chance to make eye contact with our good Samaritans before they drove away.

After Willie carefully concealed Mark's car again, we all got back in Holden's Chrysler and drove away. We pulled into a tavern once for more beer, but before he even got out of the car, Robert Willie spotted someone he didn't want to encounter. "Let's get out of here!" he told Holden. So we left and drove out into the country again, on a deserted road I'd never seen before, to what was evidently Tommy Holden's place—a dilapidated little trailer back in the woods. A small padlocked fence contained two barking dogs. What yard I could see in the car headlights hadn't been mowed in ages. And there wasn't a neighbor within a mile of the place.

Inside this cockroach-infested dump, Robert Willie ushered me to a drab, tattered sofa where I sat in front of a battered old TV set with the sound turned low. As I watched the three of them smoke pot, drink beer, and fix themselves sandwiches, I concluded my situation was quickly going from bad to worse. As long as we'd been driving around there had been some hope, however remote, that something might happen and I'd have a chance to get away. Or that someone would spot me.

Now here I was imprisoned in this trailer in the middle of nowhere with not two, but three men. Not only was there less chance for escape, but there was absolutely no chance in the world that anyone could be looking for me here.

Vaccaro brought me a piece of plain bread and a glass of water. "Have some jail food," he said, laughing.

"Better'n any jail food I ever got," Willie cracked and they all laughed.

I stared at the television long enough to realize there was some murder mystery movie showing. I tuned it out mentally even as I thought, *I hope that doesn't give them any ideas*. When I looked up again Tommy Holden had passed out from the pot and the beer, and Joseph Vaccaro was telling me to come with him. "When are you going to let me go?" I asked as he led me back into one of the bedrooms. "I want to go home." On the verge of tears, I remembered the distress my crying had created for Vaccaro early that morning. Not wanting to risk another violent, unpredictable reaction, I gulped back my tears. But I still believed Vaccaro was my best chance to talk my way out.

His expression turned very serious. "Willie says we can't let you go until I have sex with you. He doesn't want to be the only one."

"No," I told him. "Not again."

"C'mon, let's just get it over with," he said.

"You don't really want to do this," I told him. "You could just shut the door and pretend. Then you could tell him you did it. He wouldn't know."

"He wants the door left open so he can hear," he said reaching for me.

I tried to push him away. "No. Don't do this! Not again."

By this time Vaccaro was acting frantic and panicky. He pushed me down on the bed, pulled off my muddy clothes, and raped me.

Afterwards, when I was dressed again, he led me back out into the living room and made me lie down on the floor beside the sofa. He and Robert Willie tied my wrists together and then looped an end of the rope around one of Willie's arms before he sprawled out on the sofa and promptly fell asleep.

I don't have any idea how long I was lying there, afraid to move and awaken my captors. I think I was even more afraid of falling asleep and somehow missing out on my chance to escape the reality of this nightmare.

I've got to stay awake and alert, I kept telling myself. If I fell asleep I felt I would lose what very little control I had. *I can't do anything if I'm asleep.*

I do remember praying, *Please God! I need you to help me figure a way out of this. Please! I know you're out there!* When I heard no answer, I remember thinking, *Is this my punishment for staying out past curfew? Was what I did really that bad, God?* Still no answer. Had I somehow failed God? Or was he failing me? *At least help me stay awake, God, please!*

However, the emotional stress and almost two days without sleep took its toll. At some point, I drifted off. It seemed only for an instant, but the next thing I was vaguely aware of was the feel of someone gently rubbing my neck and my back. Still groggy with sleep, I tried to roll away. Then I felt someone softly brushing my face. Suddenly I was wide awake and crying. "No, get away! Not again!"

"Hey, babe. I give you a ride, feed you, and let you spend the night in my place. I'd think you'd be willing to show me a little gratitude." I opened my eyes to see Tommy Holden beside me on the floor.

"Just take me out in the woods and kill me," I screamed. "I'm not going through this again. You're gonna kill me anyway. Let's get it over with. Just take me out in the woods right now and kill me!"

Willie was stirring and Holden was on his feet and backing away in genuine surprise. "What's wrong with this chick? She's freakin' out. No one's gonna kill you, girl. What you talkin' crazy like that for?" And then, as if he'd just seen me, really seen me, for the first time, he asked. "How old is this chick? She's freakin' out or somethin'!"

When I told him I was sixteen, he reacted with alarm. "Oh, man! We gotta get her home!"

Quite obviously, it was suddenly dawning on Tommy Holden that something was happening he didn't understand—that I wasn't just someone Willie and Vaccaro picked up in some bar. Whatever was going on, he didn't want me there in his trailer. "We gotta take her home, man!"

"Okay, okay," Robert Willie obviously wasn't happy to be awakened like that at 4:30 in the morning. "We'll take her home."

"Good," Holden said, desperately trying to think the whole thing through. "But we gotta go get her car first."

"We can't let her take the car," Willie told him.

There was obviously more Holden was trying to absorb. "Why not?"

"It's evidence man. We gotta burn it."

Holden was getting more and more nervous. "All I know is, I don't want her here. We gotta take her home now!"

It was still dark when we all left Tommy Holden's trailer and got in his New Yorker again. Willie and Vaccaro were carrying their guns out in the open, which seemed to upset Holden all the more. *At least he's beginning to grasp the situation,* I thought.

"Let's just take her home right now," Holden suggested once we were on the road.

"We got to burn the car first!" Willie insisted.

"Okay, okay," Holden conceded quickly. After all, Willie had the gun.

But when we reached the power lines crossing River Road and found Mark's T-bird, Willie decided, "We're gonna need more gas to burn the car. I'll wait here with her while you two go get some gasoline. And get something for breakfast while you're at it. I'm gettin hungry."

My first thought was, *Oh, God, please don't leave me here alone with Robert Willie.* Then I decided that might be my best hope. *Holden knows the score now. Vaccaro won't be able to stop him from going right in to town and alerting the police. There will be a SWAT team out here in no time.* I began to think through what I'd do to protect myself in a showdown, to steel myself to be ready when some police sharpshooter blew Robert Willie's brains out. *That would be fine with me!*

I listened intently for the sound of impending rescue. I was poised to dive for cover at the first sound of warning. Darkness faded until the gray shadows of dawn gave way to the faintest of morning color on the treetops.

In the distance I heard the crunch of tires on gravel —louder, nearer. Holden's Chrysler. That was it. I couldn't believe it. Holden and Vaccaro hadn't returned with the police. They'd brought Twinkies, chips, and a two-gallon can full of gas.

I sat in Mark's car with the door open as they went off a ways to discuss their plans. Holden was insisting, "We gotta take the girl home." Vaccaro seemed inclined to agree.

"Are you crazy?" Willie argued. "We cannot take her home!"

"I don't know what we should do," Vaccaro admitted.

"Joe," Willie turned to his partner. "You know very well there is no way we can take that girl home!"

"Why not?" Holden demanded to know.

I couldn't make out the next exchange, but whatever Willie said upset Holden and he walked back toward the cars. Toward me.

"They don't want to take me home, do they?" I asked.

"No," Tommy Holden admitted.

"They want to kill me, don't they?"

"Yeah. But don't worry. They're not gonna kill you. I won't let 'em. I told 'em they'd have to kill me first."

"You think that'll stop them?" I said, "Ask them what they did to my boyfriend."

"What?"

"Ask them. They kidnapped us, took my boyfriend out in the woods, and dumped him. I heard two shots. I don't know what they did to him. Ask them!"

Holden was panicking now. He rushed back toward Willie and Vaccaro. "What are y'all planning to do?" he asked.

"You askin' me what we need to do? I'm sayin' we lock her in the trunk and set the car on fire," Willie told him.

When I heard that, I experienced a split second of absolute terror. I couldn't imagine a more terrible fate than being burned alive while locked in the trunk of a car. The next instant I determined there was no way I was going to die like that. Those guys weren't big enough or strong enough to lock me in the trunk and set me on fire. They would have to kill me first.

With that realization came a sense of peace. *They may kill me. But if they do, it won't be on their terms. It will be on mine.* I bent over and slipped off my sandals so I could get better traction to run. I rolled up my jeans so I wouldn't trip on the flared legs. And then I slid to the edge of the seat and placed my feet on the ground.

Muscles tensed, I was ready to run. When I heard Robert Willie say, "Fine. We'll take her home then. But I tell ya, we're making a big mistake. We're all gonna end up in prison over this!"

I froze and they all started back toward Mark's car. *Too late to run.*

"Ya gonna be cool about this, ain't ya?" Willie asked as we drove toward Madisonville in the old Chrysler. "You're not gonna go crazy and call the cops now, are you? 'Cause we're bein' nice. We ain't *gotta* let you go. We've had a fun coupla days and there's no need to bring in any cops, right?"

"I don't care about the police," I told him. "I just want to be with my family again."

"Good," Willie said. "Because we know where you live now. And if you go to the cops, we're gonna have to come back and kill your sister."

"Okay," I said, watching the road ahead and realizing we were fast approaching Madisonville.

"You can just tell your folks you went off for a couple days with some friends, okay?"

"Okay."

"So we're cool. We're friends?"

"Sure."

"We know some of the same people. We're bound to run into each other from time to time. If we do, we're cool, right? Like if I saw you on the street sometime, I could come over and we could talk, right?"

I wasn't ready to go that far. "That might make people suspicious. I think it would be better to pretend we didn't even know each other."

"You're probably right. That would be best," he admitted, before he added, "You know I'm doing this 'cause I love you."

I thought, *You're the same guy who was wanting to burn me up just minutes ago. This is totally insane.* But I didn't say anything because I could see Bayou Desire and the city limits of Madisonville just ahead. *Are they really going to let me go this time?*

They stopped and let me out near the cemetery at the outskirts of town. I had my purse, Mark's tape case of music they'd let me take out of his car, along with a big sea shell I'd given Mark from a beach in Florida. My arms were full as I began walking slowly toward town.

I listened for the sound of the car, but I forced myself not to run or make any sudden moves that might change their minds. I couldn't believe they were letting me go. *They are going to pull up beside me any minute, drag me back in the car, and laugh at me like they did so many times before. Or they are going to let me get a little ways down the road so they can run me down and kill me with the car.*

I flinched when I heard tires squeal as the big Chrysler took off and roared toward me. *Let them run me down. At least it will be over with.* I didn't look back. I tensed for the impact.

But the car accelerated right on past me.

They're going to stop any second.

But they didn't. Instead, the car disappeared around the curve going into Madisonville and continued out of sight.

I kept walking. Around the curve now, and there, a little more than a block ahead of me, I saw my Uncle Allen pull into the parking lot to open up his grocery store for the morning.

That's when I began to run.

CHAPTER SEVEN

"Where's Mark?"

The store was still locked when I got there. Through the front door, I could see my uncle in the back, starting his morning chores. I pounded violently on the glass and shouted, "Let me in! Uncle Allen! Let me in!"

He looked up at the commotion. I pounded again.

I knew he couldn't hear what I was shouting. But I kept shouting anyway.

My clothes were covered with mud. My hair was tangled and matted. I was such a mess that my own uncle didn't recognize me at first. I could tell that by the questioning expression on his face as he walked from the back of the store.

I remember seeing the recognition and surprise finally register just before he reached the door and began to unlock it "Debbie! Where have you been? Everyone's been looking for you!"

"Just let me in!" I said, pressing past him. "Then bolt the door and don't open it for anyone!"

"What's going on?"

"Hurry! Over behind the counter and get down out of sight! They could be back any minute."

I rushed past the checkout counter, grabbed a phone, and crouched down. Uncle Allen followed and asked, "Debbie, are you in some kind of trouble?"

"I can't talk," I said. "I gotta call home!"

My mother picked up on the first ring. "Debbie?" I could hear the desperation in her voice.

"Mom?" I heard her gasp. "It's me."

"I know," she said. "Where are you, Debbie? Where are you?"

"I'm over at the store. I need you to come and get me right now. Don't tell anybody I'm here. Just come and get me."

"I'm on the way!"

We lived only two blocks away. When she drove into the parking lot less than two minutes later, I sprinted out of the store to the car and flung open the car door. At the exact same time we both asked, "Where's Mark?"

Until I heard those words come out of Mom's mouth, I'd been hoping against hope that Mark was okay. That the kidnappers had been telling the truth

when they said they released him. That he would probably beat me home.

"Oh, Mom," I began to cry. "They've done something terrible to him!"

"Who? Debbie, what has happened?"

"We were kidnapped! They left Mark somewhere ...
I heard shots."

"I knew something was wrong! I just knew it!" She was
beginning to get hysterical. "I was trying to tell peo ..."

"Mom!" I interrupted. "Where are David and Dionne?"

"David's gone camping with the Carter family.
Dionne went on to your dad's house."

"Good, because they know I have a brother and sister. And they said if I told anyone what happened, they
would kill Dionne."

"Oh my God!" Mom began shaking.

"Let's just get home!"

I bolted from the car across the yard to our trailer. Mom
was right behind me. "What are we going to do?" she
asked as soon as we got inside and slammed the door
behind us.

"I've got to call the police," I told her. "But first
we've got to make sure the doors and all the windows
are locked. They know where I live."

Mom ran frantically from room to room, checking
locks. I dialed my father's house in Mississippi to make
sure my brother and sister were all right. My stepmother, Brenda, was relieved to hear my voice; she said
Dad was out with one of my uncles searching for me.

"Where's Dionne?" I asked.

"Right here."

"Don't let her out of the house!" I told my stepmother I'd explain later and hung up.

"We need to call Poppie and Mimi," Mom said as she took the phone and dialed.

"Debbie's here," was all she had to say. Then, "Okay."

I knew my grandparents would be over within a minute. "I gotta call the police," I said. "I don't know what they did to Mark!"

I dialed the sheriff's office myself. One of my best friends' mother worked there, so I knew the number by heart. "My name is Debbie Cuevas," I told the person who answered. "My mom has been to your office and made a number of phone calls to tell you that I was missing. Well, I was kidnapped. I just got home and I think you need to send a couple deputies over here right away." I gave them the address and hung up.

My grandparents had arrived. Mom had let them in and was telling them I'd been kidnapped. Mimi was crying. But it was Poppie, who hadn't been well recently, whose reaction I worried about most. He turned so white that it scared me. Yet he promptly announced, "I'm gonna get my shotgun." Then he ran back to the house and returned moments later carrying a twelve-gauge.

"We gotta call Mark's parents," I said. But I didn't know what to say to them.

So Mom made that call. "Mary, this is Sharon. Debbie's here! I think you need to come over."

Where's Mark? I could tell by the pained way Mom looked at me that was the response she heard from the other end.

"We don't know," I heard Mom reply. "We've called the police and I think you need to get over here."

Less than five minutes later, Mary and Johnny Brewster arrived. "What happened?" they wanted to know.

"We were kidnapped," I said. "They drove us to Alabama. That's where they let Mark go." Mark's mom began crying. His father was visibly upset. I felt terrible being the one to give them such news. I deliberately didn't mention the gunshots.

The Brewsters naturally wanted to know the details: when, where, who? Before I could begin to answer, two uniformed sheriff's deputies arrived at the front door.

I knew Mom had been talking to the police ever since Saturday morning, when she realized I hadn't come home the night before. That's when Mark's mom had called, concerned that Mark hadn't come home, and they first realized we were both missing. The very first thing Mom did was to drive out to Lake Ramsey, where a number of Madisonville families had gone camping for the weekend. She remembered me telling her Mark and I might be driving out to the campground to see some of our friends; she thought maybe she'd just gotten her signals crossed and we'd actually planned to spend the night camping with friends. But when she didn't find us there and no one at the park had even seen us Friday night, she became very alarmed. She drove straight to the sheriff's office in a panic to tell them her daughter was missing—that I'd gone out on a date and had not returned.

The police brushed her off. "This kind of thing happens all the time. She'll probably be home soon." They said there was nothing they could do; since I was sixteen years old, I had to be gone for seventy-two hours before they could officially list me as "missing" and put out an all points bulletin. "She'll turn up by then," they assured Mom. "Kids probably decided to run off and get married or something. Happens all the time."

"You don't know my daughter," Mom told them. "Debbie wouldn't want to worry me or her grandparents. She would never do anything like that."

"We hear that all the time, too," they told her.

The next time Mom talked to the police she told them she'd searched my room. That she knew I couldn't have run off with Mark, because "none of her clothes are missing. Her makeup and blow-dryer are still here. What sixteen-year-old girl is going to run off without her makeup and her hair dryer?"

"It happens," she was told.

"But she didn't even empty her money bank. If she and Mark were planning to run off, she wouldn't have left her money."

The police still hadn't been convinced. "When she comes home, it'll all make sense."

No matter what the police thought, my mother wasn't going to wait seventy-two hours to mount her own search. She and Mark's family called everyone they could think of who might have seen us or know what happened. Local hospitals. Friends. "Maybe they went parking somewhere and then just fell asleep," someone speculated.

"Debbie doesn't go parking," Mom replied. Even so, she and other members of the family had driven around to all the local lovers lanes and popular teenage parking spots Saturday morning. Nothing. Yet each time she'd called the sheriff's office she'd been told the same thing: "Give it time."

I don't know how much of this the two deputies in our living room knew. But they very matter-of-factly instructed, "Tell us what happened."

"You've got to find Mark," I said.

"Let's start at the beginning," said one deputy, as he pulled out his notebook.

"But I know right where they let Mark go over in Alabama. I know their names. I even know where you can catch them right now. Just before they let me go they were planning to take Mark's car to Fitzsimmon's Road and burn it. I heard them talking. If you go there right now you can catch them."

"First we need to get the whole story," the second deputy insisted.

I felt like screaming. Instead, I started talking as fast as I could. I told them about the riverfront, the two guys with guns, how they stowed Mark in the trunk . . . .

"We need to find Mark! He could be hurt!"

"Why would you think that?" they pressed.

I didn't want to say anything that would further alarm Mark's parents. "Can't you just call someone to go look for him? I know where they let him go. He could be hurt!"

"You keep saying that. Why?"

"Because . . ." I didn't have any choice but to come right out and say it. "Because I heard gunshots and . . ." Mary Brewster really lost it at that point.

One of the deputies looked to the other and then back at me: "I hope you understand the serious nature of what you're saying; the seriousness of lying to officers of the law."

"You think I'm lying?" I asked, incredulous. "Just look at me." In the long seconds of awkward silence that followed, I heard my mother and Mark's mom sobbing. "Ask anyone who knows me," I challenged them. "They'll tell you I wouldn't ever lie about something like this!"

"Well," the first deputy said, "Sometimes teenagers decide to run off together and then they change their minds and co . . . ."

"That's it!" I'd had enough. I was furious. "Get out of my house!"

"Now, Miss," the second deputy began in a patronizing tone. "There's no need to get upset. You . . ."

"No! You get out! Both of you!" I was yelling at them. I turned to Mom, "Call someone else!" I wanted someone who would listen.

"This isn't going to get us anywhere," one of the cops was saying. "We need to hear the rest of the story."

I marched to the front door and opened it. "GET OUT OF MY HOUSE!" I screamed. "RIGHT NOW!"

As I motioned out the door I saw our local Madisonville police officer approaching the trailer. "Elroy!" I exclaimed in welcome relief. Like most kids in town, I'd known Officer Badon (everyone called him Elroy) most of my life. He was a friendly, approachable, thirty-something black man who'd quickly earned the respect of the townspeople when he'd taken over as Madisonville's one-man police force after long-time town cop Spike Turney retired several years before.

"Debbie, what happened to you? Where have you been?" Elroy asked.

"Mark and I were kidnapped, Elroy!" I blurted out. Motioning toward the deputies I said, "These men won't believe me and we gotta find Mark because . . . ."

"Okay, okay," Elroy patted my arm. "Settle down a minute. I believe you!" He turned toward the deputies. "If this young lady says she was kidnapped, then she was!"

Relieved to finally have a listener, I grabbed his arm. "Elroy, I know who it was. I know their names. I know details. I know right where they left Mark. And these guys won't listen to any of that—they just want me to start at the beginning and tell them the entire story. Meantime Mark could be lying out in the woods hurt or . . . worse."

Elroy stopped me. "What were their names?"

"Robert Lee Willie and Joe somebody."

"How do you know that?" one of the deputies suddenly wanted to know.

"Robert Willie showed me some parole papers or something with his name on them. It even had his birthdate—January 2, 1958."

"Oh my God!" the deputy exclaimed to his partner. "She's telling the truth!" They knew Robert Willie's name.

"I think we better get some more people over here," Elroy said. The deputies concurred and one of them rushed out to call their office.

"Did they . . . uh . . . do anything besides kidnap you?" the remaining deputy asked.

"Yeah," I said.

"Did they rape you?"

I nodded. "Yeah." My mom, my grandmother, and Mary Brewster were all crying now.

"We need to notify the hospital we'll be coming in for an exam," the deputy decided.

"Can I take a shower?" I asked. I was still covered with mud and I felt filthy.

They said I could. Perhaps they felt so sorry for me, so guilty about not believing me at first, that they forgot procedures and didn't think about the evidence I might be washing away.

Everything was happening so fast. It had only been a half hour or so since Mom and I got home. The entire time in the trailer had been one chaotic blur. Now we were being whisked away and raced by patrol car to the sheriff's office up in Covington. The whole time I was thinking, *They have got to find Mark!*

That's what I kept trying to tell the deputies as they attempted to take a formal statement. "I know where he is! I know right where they let him go!"

Still, the police wanted to hear the entire story first. From the beginning.

I finally refused to talk. "I'm not saying another word until you try to find Mark!"

"Get the Alabama state police on the radio," someone said. Once they established contact, I began giving directions to Wilcox Road off Interstate 10. The deputy repeated what I was saying to the Alabama authorities on the other end of the link. But the step-by-step relay of directions back and forth got so awkward they finally put me on the radio to talk directly to the Alabama officer. He not only knew the exit, he knew the convenience store and the service road I told him about. He even sounded familiar with the turnoff into the woods when I described it. He promised they'd send someone to check the area right away.

Relieved that someone was finally looking for Mark, I began a thorough account for the police—describing everything I could remember. Every detail I had told myself during the ordeal that I *have to remember, so they can put these guys away*. It was a very long statement.

Mom was asked to wait outside the room where I was talking to the cops. She told me later that at one point she overheard a couple of the men coming out of the room. "That's a pretty incredible story," one of them was saying.

"Maybe," the other one agreed. "But I know the family. That girl is telling the truth."

Worried for me and also concerned that some people still seemed unwilling to accept everything I was saying, Mom was glad she had called Jeff Bratton just before we'd left home. Mr. Bratton was the father of my best friend Kay Bratton, and also a lawyer. He had rushed to the sheriff's office, arriving just before we did, and sat in the room with me as I made my statement.

My own father also caught up with us about that time. The deputies let me go out to see him as soon as he arrived. He hugged me desperately as I kept telling him, "I'm okay. I'm okay."

Daddy hadn't really believed that Mark and I had run off together. But so many people had speculated about the possibility that he recruited his brother and the two of them had been driving along the Mississippi coast from Biloxi to Gulfport, frantically searching the parking lots of every beachfront hotel and motel they came to. He'd realized it was a desperate, probably futile quest, but he had to do something, if it was only looking for Mark's car.

Mark's car! I told the deputies again that I knew where the kidnappers had been going right after they let me go. They'd planned to move the T-Bird to Fitzsimmons Road to burn the evidence.

I never did know how long it was before they sent anyone out to look. But when they did, they found the car abandoned along the side of Fitzsimmon's Road at a curve—still smoldering.

I do know that it was a little later that Sunday morning, when I'd finished my first statement, that deputies drove me to nearby St. Tammany Parish Hospital where it seemed like forever before they located an OB-GYN to conduct an exam.

By the time that was over, someone had decided there was a chance I could help in the search for Mark. So I climbed in the back of the patrol car between my mom and dad. Detective Herman drove, and another deputy sat in front, asking me more questions, as we headed for Alabama.

We stopped briefly at a Popeye's Fried Chicken drive-thru in Slidell to get me something to eat. Having gone without a meal since Friday night, I was suddenly famished. From there we headed across Mississippi for

Alabama, lights flashing, at speeds of over a hundred miles an hour.

At one point, when I said something hopeful about Mark, I saw the knowing look the deputies gave Mom, like they were warning her not to let me get my hopes up. Clearly, they didn't expect to find Mark alive. That distressed me.

Somewhere east of Mobile we met an ambulance heading the opposite way, its siren screaming, its lights pulsing. I wondered, *Could that be Mark?*

A few minutes later, we received notification that Mark had been found. He had indeed been shot. But he was still alive. They were rushing him to a hospital at that very moment. *Mark probably was in that ambulance.* That was all we could learn about him right then, but the Alabama authorities definitely wanted to talk to me. Immediately.

Detective Herman stopped at the police station in the nearest small town. The Alabama state police took a brief statement about the part of the story that took place in their jurisdiction. But when we received official notice that Mark was being admitted to a hospital back in Mobile, we quickly got back in the sheriff's car and headed there.

Mark's entire family had gathered in the emergency room by the time we arrived. His parents, his three brothers, plus other relatives and friends.

"Mark's alive!" his mom greeted me, crying. "He's alive!" His parents filled us in. He'd been shot in the head. He was being prepared for surgery to remove the bullet. Doctors had told them Mark was expected to live.

The Alabama police found him right where I'd told them to look. He'd been lying on the ground not a hundred feet from the tree where Willie and Vaccaro had tied him up. His wrists were still tied with his own shoelaces, but he'd chewed through the cord that had bound him to the tree. He was barely conscious when the Alabama troopers found him, his eyes open and darting around in fear and shock. Buzzards circled overhead.

Mark had been covered with blood. He'd been stabbed in the side with a knife. There were four more cuts across his neck, none of them deep enough to penetrate his trachea or reach his jugular. Evidently those wounds had been intended not to kill, but to torture him. There were also a couple cigarette burns over his ribs. He'd been shot once, at close range, in the back of the head.

I wanted to see him, but the doctors wouldn't let me into intensive care because I wasn't a relative. Even when the Brewster family pressed them, the doctors wouldn't budge.

Mark's older brother, Johnny, went in to tell him, "Debbie's here. She's okay." When he heard that, Mark jerked and tried to say something—the first voluntary response the doctors had witnessed since he'd been admitted. "Did you see that?" Johnny asked them. "He wants to see her. You need to let Debbie in so he can see her. He needs that."

The doctors finally conceded, but not until they tried to prepare me for what I was going to see and warned me against any emotional reactions. They didn't want Mark upset.

My knees felt like jello as I entered the room. The moment he saw me, silent tears started running down Mark's face. Despite all the "Don't get upset in front of him" warnings, I cried too, as he reached out awkwardly toward me with his left hand. The doctors had explained that his entire right side seemed to be paralyzed.

I couldn't see the bullet wound at the back of his head. But the bandage on his side and the ugly red cigarette burn marks were visible. So were the four slashes on his neck. I'd expected all that. What I wasn't prepared for was the angry red swelling from hundreds of ant bites that covered half of his body. He'd crawled into a fire ant nest and hadn't been able to get out or brush off their vicious swarming attack. He looked terrible.

"I'm okay," I told Mark through my tears. "And the doctors who are going to operate on you say you're going to be fine, too." He squeezed my hand. Then he reached up with his left hand and gently stroked my neck.

Looking down at his neck, I realized what he was doing and assured him, "I'm okay. They didn't cut me." He tugged at the edge of my shirt and I lifted it to show him my side—that I hadn't been stabbed like he was. "They didn't do that to me either," I assured him again. "I really am fine."

Tears flowed down his cheeks again. I stayed just a little longer, trying to convince him that I truly was okay and that he was going to recover as well.

Then my time was up and I had to leave. Outside in the corridor, the shock and horror of everything that happened over the past forty-eight hours suddenly became overwhelmingly real. I collapsed into the arms of my dad and wept as Mom and several of the Brewsters quickly gathered around trying to assure me, "Everything's gonna be all right. Mark's gonna come through this!"

Yet Mark's entire family acted devastated. His mom was sobbing uncontrollably in the waiting room. His brothers paced around not knowing what to do. Worried. Frustrated. Furious. At one point, Johnny punched a concrete wall so hard I was afraid he'd broken his hand.

I too was walking back and forth, so obviously distressed, so wired, that the hospital staff wanted to admit me—to the psychiatric ward. When I heard that I said, "No way! If you want to get me a regular bed where I can lie down and get some sleep, fine. Just not in the pysch ward." I did agree to take some Valium they gave me.

Then I went outside to doze in the back seat of Mark's uncle's car, which they pulled up close to the emergency room doors, where they could keep an eye on me.

The surgeons termed Mark's surgery a "success." They weren't able to remove the bullet, but they said it presented no further danger where it lodged in his skull. They did extract some skull fragments that had shattered and penetrated into the brain, causing the swelling that was affecting his speech and paralyzing his right side. What damage remained was not considered life threatening. The doctors did say the next six months would be critical to Mark's recovery. But they were hopeful that with hard work and proper therapy he could regain most, maybe even everything, he'd lost.

The deputies who'd brought us headed back late that evening, but my parents and I spent Sunday night at the hospital. Monday morning we received a phone call saying the FBI and the sheriff's departments in both St. Tammany and Washington Parishes wanted more information from me. So we said our reluctant good-byes to Mark's family and started home.

As Dad drove us back toward Louisiana, my troubled mind raced—replaying everything that had happened and wondering what lay ahead. As glad as I was that Mark was alive, I remained both worried and scared.

No one could be sure yet how completely Mark would recover. And the police still hadn't located Robert Willie, Joseph Vaccaro, or even Tommy Holden.

Somehow, even then, I realized the ordeal was far from over.

CHAPTER EIGHT

Making the Case

Even before we left the hospital in Mobile, the sheriff's deputies had approached Mom to say, "We're gonna need your daughter's help to make this case."

Once we got home they said the same thing to me, "We're gonna need your help." But it was voiced almost apologetically. As if they thought they might need to persuade me to cooperate. As if I might not want to. Or maybe they were just worried that I wouldn't be able to talk about what had happened.

They didn't understand just how desperately I *wanted* to help. From that moment during the very first rape when I vowed that I was not only going to survive, I was going to remember every possible significant detail, I'd been living for this chance to help the authorities. I would do anything to make sure the men who'd done this to Mark and me would be caught and punished.

"Okay," I said. "What do you need me to do?"

The police didn't ask much on Monday. I was too exhausted—emotionally and physically—after three straight nights without sleep. So, very soon after we got back to St. Tammany Parish, they sent me home to get some rest.

Actually, I spent the night with my aunt and uncle who lived in a gated community with good security. The police, too, promised to keep an eye on me. As long as Robert Willie and Joseph Vaccaro were still on the loose, none of us thought it was safe for me to stay at home or with my grandparents.

I felt more like myself by Tuesday morning when a deputy showed up to drive Mom and me back to the sheriff's office to go over everything again with investigators. There an assistant district attorney told me, as the deputies had the day before, "We're gonna need your help, Debbie."

I was still adding details to my previous statement when the FBI showed up. After Special Agent Grover Leap walked in and introduced himself and two of his colleagues to the local authorities, there was a very noticeable change of atmosphere in the room. Without anyone ever saying so, it was clear to me that the FBI was suddenly very much in charge. Their unspoken attitude came through loud and clear: *While a case like this may seem shocking and unusual here in St. Tammany Parish, we've seen a lot of kidnappings elsewhere.* Not that they acted as if this was all simply routine, but their very presence and their matter-of-fact, here's-what-we're-gonna-do approach seemed to bring an immediate sense of focus and direction in that room, which made me feel safer and more confident that my kidnappers would soon be caught.

The FBI also told me, "We're going to need your help."

I spent much of that Tuesday with the authorities, driving around St. Tammany and Washington Parishes, trying to retrace, as closely as possible, everywhere the kidnappers had taken me.

I went back to the riverfront for the first time since Friday night to show the police where it all began. What had always been a peaceful place full of warm remembrances now felt forever connected to a chillingly vivid nightmare of guns, violence, pain, and fear.

I showed them where we went right after Mark and I were kidnapped—out the Turnpike Highway to where we turned on Tantilla Ranch Road. When the caravan of police cars stopped, we got out there. I looked around carefully, trying to concentrate. Everything appeared different in the daylight. But this was indeed the place.

"This is where they put Mark in the trunk?"

"Yes," I replied.

"And this is where Robert Willie told you to take off your clothes and forced you to have sex?" The question was asked cautiously, as if they were afraid I might suddenly fall apart.

"The first time was when we were driving away from here. Joseph Vaccaro was driving." I was afraid they were going to ask me to recount the details of the rape itself again. But they didn't.

We retraced the roads the kidnappers had taken on our roundabout trek to the Mississippi border. Then we turned and tried to follow the route I'd traveled with the kidnappers when we'd returned to Louisiana on Saturday afternoon—which was harder because we'd wandered up and down so many unmarked country roads.

Whenever we reached a familiar looking spot, the cars stopped for me to get my bearings. As the day wore on I began to feel like the central character in some television or movie drama. Each time I got out of the patrol car, everyone in the other cars—the FBI agents, the other deputies, and the DA's investigators—would gather round to ask questions or just listen to what I remembered about that particular place. A photographer would take pictures.

The sheriff's detectives seemed especially interested when I directed them to turn off the main highway between Folsom and Franklinton onto a gravel roadway marked by a sign that said "Fricke Rd."

"You came here with Willie and Vaccaro?" they wanted to know.

"I couldn't read the sign Saturday. But I'm pretty sure this is the road," I told them, studying the terrain as we went deeper and deeper into the woods. I knew why they were so interested.

On Monday, when I'd described this place to investigators, one of them turned to the other and said, "That sounds like the road to Fricke's Cave where they found the Hathaway girl's purse."

"There was another girl kidnapped?" I asked.

"We don't know that," one of the men replied. "But she's been missing for almost a week and on Saturday some picnickers out to Fricke's Cave found her purse in the woods. We sent out a search party but they didn't turn up anything else. "

We'd gone on talking about my experience and I hadn't thought any more about the missing girl until I saw the "Fricke Rd." sign. Obviously, the deputies thought there might be some connection between the two cases. However, I was too busy looking for familiar landmarks to give that much thought.

I remember the road turning like this. "Yeah, I'm pretty sure we drove out here," I told the deputies.

As I watched the road narrow and swampy woodlands close in around us, a wave of uneasiness went right through me. This was definitely the place.

"Right about here is where we saw an old black gentleman and a young boy carrying cane fishing poles," I told the authorities at one particularly desolate spot in the road. Yet I wondered, *Where did the old man and his grandson come from? And where did they go?*

When we finally reached the end of the road, there were a couple vehicles, including a sheriff's patrol car, already parked there. I showed my escorts where Willie had turned around and right where he'd parked Mark's car. So we stopped and everyone got out again.

One of the deputies who'd been there when we arrived walked over to our group and pulled a couple of his colleagues aside. I couldn't make out everything that was said, but I overheard enough to learn that Faith Hathaway's mother and stepfather, Elizabeth and Vernon Harvey, had come there to search for their daughter themselves. And they'd brought along a psychic to help them find her. But the deputy said they were about ready to give up and head home.

I remember a strange chill running up my spine as I eavesdropped on their conversation. I was never sure if that sensation had been triggered by the mention of a psychic or if the dark and foreboding feel of that spot prompted some sort of sensory flashback. But I couldn't help feeling, *Something terrible has happened to that girl.*

As the other two cars pulled out, I once again put the Hathaway case out my mind. I was too busy trying to sort out my own memories. For the first time all day, I felt a little confused. I'd been so sure that when Joseph Vaccaro had walked off into the woods and left me alone with Robert Willie, there had been a gate in a fence nearby. And this certainly looked like that place. The police were noting the tire tracks right where I said they had turned Mark's car around. This had to be the place. Yet there was no gate. No fence either.

I worried that if the cops thought I was wrong about the gate, they might question other parts of my story as well. But they didn't seem concerned about the discrepancy. We'd traveled down so many secluded roads they figured I was remembering the gate and the fence from some other location. But the confusion and uncertainty bothered me. I wanted to be absolutely sure. I wanted all the facts to fit. I wanted people to believe me.

After we left the Fricke's Cave area, my police escort and I spent a considerable amount of time zigzagging over more back roads in search of convenience stores and bars where Willie and Vaccaro had stopped to buy beer and snacks on Saturday afternoon. At each place we found, the investigators would go in to ask if anyone there had seen the kidnappers. Time after time I was disappointed when they found no one who remembered seeing Willie or Vaccaro on Saturday afternoon.

But my worst moments of the entire day came when we drove out to Bennett Bridge Road to find Tommy Holden's trailer. Seeing the place again, even in daylight, brought back a memory flood of horror. I refused to (actually I just couldn't) make myself get out of the car. Holden was long gone. No one was home. The police acquired a search warrant and spent quite a while inside looking around and gathering any evidence they could find.

My best friend, Kay Bratton, spent the night with me Tuesday evening. When her dad had heard my story on Sunday, he and Kay's mom decided to fly their daughter home from church camp in the North Carolina mountains so she could be with me. As happy as I was to see Kay, as hard as I hugged her when she showed up on my aunt and uncle's doorstep, I felt really bad that she'd had to leave camp before the week had really gotten started. This annual camp trip was always a highlight of the year for our entire church youth group.

Kay brushed off my apologies that she'd had to come home early by joking: "You know I must love you. If I didn't, I sure wouldn't fly in the weather we went through today. Why, I turbulated all the way from Atlanta to New Orleans just for you."

I had to laugh. One of the things I loved about Kay was her playful and creative use of language. Her sense of humor. Her loyalty. Her . . . well . . . her friendship. We'd been best friends since fourth grade. And there was no one in the world I would have chosen over Kay Bratton to be with me.

Her dad had obviously filled Kay in with the broad strokes. She let me know she'd be willing to listen to anything I wanted or needed to say. But she didn't pry. So we didn't talk in much detail about the ordeal I'd been through. Mostly she was there to remember, talk, and laugh about everything two sixteen-year-olds remember, talk, and laugh about with their best friends.

In the aftermath of the most unimaginable nightmare of my life, in the midst of this police drama where I'd been playing the main character all day long, Kay Bratton provided an island of normality, a touchpoint with my real world. When I was with her I could just relax and be the person I'd always been. And I desperately needed the chance to do that.

Wednesday Mom and I went back to the sheriff's office in Covington for yet more backtracking. We went to the spot on River Road where they'd hidden Mark's car. And we spent quite a bit more time that day trying to find collaborating witnesses. I kept suggesting we stop at the house on River Road that had the big yard party on

Saturday, to get names of people who might have noticed me one of the times we drove by there in Mark's car. I still wanted someone, anyone to verify my story.

The police kept insisting that wasn't going to be necessary. "We believe you, Debbie. And we've got plenty of evidence already," they assured me. In addition to my testimony and Mark's, they had also found the white pickup Willie and Vaccaro had driven to the riverfront. It belonged to Robert Willie's stepfather. And they'd found a blood-stained knife behind the driver's seat.

There were two big developments that Wednesday. I was out in a sheriff's patrol car when a call came over the radio reporting that a woman's body had been found in the woods near Fricke's Cave. A young investigator with the DA's office, Mike Varnado, after going in the group with me out to Fricke Road the day before, decided to return to the area and conduct his own search. He found the body less than a hundred yards from where we had parked at the end of the road. The body was badly decomposed, but the initial description fit the missing teenager, Faith Hathaway. The body was naked. She was lying on her back, covered in blood, her legs spread-eagled, with multiple vicious stab wounds to the neck and throat.

As soon as I heard those first sketchy details of the murder scene, I realized, *That's exactly what Joseph Vaccaro was describing when he was acting so strange and rambling on about their "last girlfriend." That's what he was talking about! They murdered Faith Hathaway!*

I think I felt more afraid at that moment than I had at any point during the kidnapping itself. I knew what they'd done to Mark, of course. But that was the first I ever let it sink in what they were capable of. *They really had been planning to kill me when they took me out on Fricke Road. They would have done it.*

Suddenly I wanted to go back to the safety of the sheriff's office. I didn't want to be wandering around in the backwoods anymore looking for places two murderers had taken me. Two murderers who had threatened me and were still on the loose.

The second development came later that same day. I don't remember exactly where we were or what we were doing, but I was still with some of the sheriff's people when we got a call. Willie, Vaccaro, and Holden had all been arrested up in Arkansas.

"Arkansas?" I couldn't believe it. They'd had no money. Tommy Holden's car wouldn't have made it to Arkansas. How would they have gotten that far away?

No one knew that yet. Maybe the details would come out once they were extradited back to Louisiana. But the sheriff confirmed the report. The Texarkana Police Department had them all in custody.

There are no words to adequately describe my sense of relief. *Maybe now it will finally be over,* I thought. But I think I knew better.

By Wednesday, when they let me in on the news about Faith Hathaway and the capture of all three guys in Arkansas, the police seemed to have quit worrying that I might crack like an eggshell at the slightest provocation. They were treating me with real respect, openly commenting on the strength I had shown both during and since the kidnapping: "Can you believe her? Have you ever seen a sixteen-year-old like Debbie? Isn't she incredible?" And they were assuring me, "With all you've been able to tell us, all the evidence we've found, this is going to be an open and shut case if there ever was one."

I'd been determined to help even before they'd asked. And I knew I had. But some of the praise I was hearing was almost embarrassing. I knew that despite my outward show of strength I didn't feel nearly as strong inside.

I was having terrible nightmares about Robert Willie whenever I tried to sleep. And even after I learned he was in custody, I still didn't feel safe—really safe—except when I was with a group of cops, helping them nail down their case against my kidnappers. So I knew even some of the "strength" they saw was nothing more than a manifestation of the fear and vulnerability I felt inside.

I was also absolutely mortified by the press coverage the story received both in the New Orleans media and locally. Most reports referred to me only as "a sixteen-year-old girl from Madisonville." The one television station that reported my name received an angry phone call from my grandfather, who informed them I was a minor and insisted that they please have the decency to protect my privacy. He also chewed out one newspaper editor for not checking his facts before publishing an embarrassing report that said the kidnapping took place on a "secluded lover's lane."

But the facts were humiliating enough. And when the papers said "a sixteen-year-old girl and her boyfriend, Mark Brewster," it wasn't as if my identity would remain a secret from anyone in Madisonville or Covington.

All the reports referred to kidnapping, rape, and attempted murder charges. And the papers treated the whole thing like one of the most sensational crime stories ever in that part of Louisiana. They quoted deputies saying we'd been driven at gunpoint to the Alabama Gulf Coast and "on the way ... the girl was raped by Willie in the car." After detailing Willie and Vaccaro's attempted murder of Mark, the paper went on to say, "According to reports, the girl was not killed at that time because only Willie had raped her and Vaccaro still wanted his chance."

But what seemed even more embarrassing to me than having so many people know I was the "sixteen-year-old girl from Madisonville," and that I'd been raped repeatedly, was having the stories include mug shots of the two kidnappers. Having people know that I'd been raped by two such seedy, despicable-looking characters felt unbearably humiliating. I wondered if my family, my friends, or any boy who might date me could ever look at me without picturing Robert Willie and Joseph Vaccaro. That thought made me ill.

All my youth group friends returned from camp that following weekend, so I went to church Sunday evening to hear them report on their experience. It was the first time I'd left the house without a police escort—or at least in the company of multiple adults—since the kidnappers had been in custody. In some ways it was an attempt on my part to do something "routine" or "normal" again.

I sat with my friends near the front of the sanctuary. But as different kids stood up in that service to talk about what they did or what they learned from their spiritually enriching week, I couldn't help thinking, *Why didn't I go this year? If only I had gone, if I'd made my spiritual life a priority! If I'd just been where God would have wanted me to be, I would have been with them in North Carolina instead of on the riverfront with Mark and none of this would have happened to me!*

The more I thought like that, the less I wanted to listen to my friends talk about how God had blessed them, how close they felt to him, how he'd answered their prayers, and given them such a wonderful and memorable week together. And the more I heard, the more conflicted I felt in my own heart.

All week I'd overheard police and FBI agents who learned the details of my story say about me, "It's a miracle she's alive!" And part of me would say, if not to them, at least to myself, "God was with me. That's the only explanation I can see." And yet *saying* that didn't mean I was *feeling* closer to God as a result. Instead I kept thinking, *If God was really the one who saved me, if he could do that, why did he let me go through the whole horrible experience in the first place?*

After the service, when we had refreshments and stood around talking, most of the kids who spoke to me acted a little uncomfortable, like they knew they should say something, but they didn't know what. I'd expected that, but it didn't make me feel any less awkward.

The strained reaction of my friends made it easier to decide to spend the next week over in Mississippi at my father's. It was the second week of the visit my sister and I had planned to spend with him anyway, before all this happened. It gave me a chance to get away from the local news coverage about the kidnapping. And Pascagoula was only a half hour away from Mobile, so I could visit Mark in the hospital every day.

The police didn't need my help that week. Willie and Vaccaro had decided to fight extradition, so Deputy Donald Sharp and DA Investigator Mike Varnado flew up to Arkansas to interrogate them about the kidnapping and Faith Hathaway's murder.

I returned home the week after that to learn that the kidnappers had implicated each other both in the Hathaway murder and the attempted murder of Mark. With Willie and Vaccaro's own statements, plus all the physical evidence they'd collected, the police assured me that there would be multiple charges and that they had what it would take to make those charges stick. But they were counting on my testimony to seal the deal, so they were still going to be needing my help as they prepared for the legal process in the weeks and months ahead.

Mark's doctors transferred him to a hospital in New Orleans just a few days later. It wasn't long before he was released from there with an optimistic prognosis for his recovery if he continued his therapy at home. I spent most of my summer either helping the police prepare their case or at Mark Brewster's home, just a couple blocks from Mimi and Poppie's.

Mark's condition reminded me a lot of how my Grandfather Cuevas had been after his stroke. Mark's speech recovery seemed to proceed even slower than his physical mobility. And his struggle to talk frustrated Mark so much we didn't communicate much. But I spent hours most days at his house, watching movies, playing cards, reading the newspaper to him, going to Covington with him for his physical therapy, coaxing him to do his speech therapy, taking him for drives when he felt desperate to get out of the house, or just sitting quietly with him at home.

I had plenty opportunity just to sit and think. I spent a lot of that time rehashing my question about why God would care enough to help Mark and me survive but not prevent us from going through such a horrible experience. Eventually that one big "why" question evolved into a long list of others:

Why did my father have to drink and create so many unpleasant scenes when I was little?

Why did our family have to go through so many financial problems?

Why did my brother and sister and I have to go through two divorces?

Why did my mother have to be out half the night on a date instead of staying home like most parents and making sure I got in on time?

The more "why" questions I came up with, the more I felt victimized, the more abandoned I felt by God, the more angry I became. Of course, I didn't voice those questions to anyone. Nor did I admit I was now too terrified to go out alone at night and that I still routinely awakened in a cold sweat from vivid nightmares about Robert Willie and Joseph Vaccaro.

When people asked me how I was doing, my immediate answer was always the same: "I'm fine." Few people ever tried to press me further than that. And there were even fewer times when I ventured a more complete or honest response.

I do remember one Sunday night, after youth group, I went out beside the church and sat in my grandparents' Chrysler Cordoba talking with a friend named Brad Morris. As long as I'd been part of the youth group, I'd been pals with Brad and his older brother Bo—a couple of outgoing, fun-loving jocks I saw only at church on Sundays and Wednesdays because they attended rival Mandeville High School. I'd had sort of a crush on Bo, but nothing came of it. They were both just friends—a couple all-American, good-guy types I enjoyed having as "buddies."

Brad hadn't seen me since the kidnapping, so he asked how I was doing. When I assured him I was fine, he actually asked me a couple questions about the kidnapping itself. I'd been by the sheriff's office earlier and just happened to have in my purse a typed copy of the first statement I'd made to the police. I handed it to Brad and said, "Here. Read this."

He did. But it was clearly more than he had wanted to know. He asked for a couple points of clarification as he read. When he finished and handed the transcript back to me, neither of us knew what to say. But by that time, Brad had missed his ride with his brother, so I volunteered to take him home. We both tried to talk about other things during the fifteen-minute drive.

I don't remember sharing the details with anyone else. I learned it was easier to act strong and just tell people, "I'm fine."

Mom wanted me to talk with a rape counselor. I refused, saying, "I don't want to! I'm fine."

We went to Texas, ostensibly to visit my uncle and aunt for a week. But I think the bigger reason was that my mother thought it would be good for me to get away from home, from the media coverage, and from everything else for a while. My Aunt Barbara, Mom's oldest brother's wife, had always been a favorite relative of mine. Quite a bit younger than my mom, she seemed more like an older cousin than an aunt from another generation. We'd always been able to talk to each other. But when she expressed genuine concern for me and asked, "How are you holding up?" I gave even her the standard reply: "I'm fine."

The truth is, I'd garnered so much respect and praise from the authorities for being strong, that I now had an image to live up to. So I had to be "fine"; it was expected.

All summer long, whenever I met with the assistant district attorneys, they kept telling me, "A big part of our case is going to depend on you." So I had to be strong for them. And if justice was to be done for Faith Hathaway, I had to continue to be "fine."

I can't count the number of days when I'd get a call from Mary Brewster saying Mark was so discouraged she couldn't get him to do his therapy. "Could you come over, Debbie? Maybe he'll do it for you." So I always had to be strong and "fine" for Mark as well.

It seemed especially important to be strong for my mother. She'd depended on my strength and responsibility as the oldest child since I was nine and she and my father had divorced. I knew she was worried about me. I realized finances were even tighter than usual because she'd taken off so many days without pay the week we had spent going over everything again with the police. So for her sake too I needed to be "fine."

Most of all, I felt I had to be strong for my grandpa. Poppie was not in good health himself. I knew how much he loved me, and that he would worry about me if he thought anything was wrong with me. So I had to be "fine" for him as well.

Oh sure, there were times when I looked at the long list of people I was being strong for and wanted to scream, "What about me?" I'd hear so many people express concern about Mark's recovery that I'd want to say, "I may not have any physical scars on the outside, but I'm hurting, too."

I didn't, however. Because every time I'd start feeling sorry for myself like that, I'd think of how Mark suffered and how Faith Hathaway died. Then I'd scold myself, *What right do you have to feel hurt?* and the guilt over feeling bad would make me feel even worse.

After weeks of preparation, the legal ordeal began in July. First on the docket were the federal charges against Willie and Vaccaro: two counts of kidnapping and another for conspiracy. Special Agent Leap and his FBI colleagues, Terry Scott and Scharlene Cartlidge, spent day after day going over every aspect of my testimony and preparing me for my first official court appearance. They even suggested I wear something "nice, but conservative" when I took the witness stand.

After agonizing over my own wardrobe to no avail, I finally settled on one of my friend Kay's outfits: a sleeveless, white, belted dress, with a full skirt. I remember feeling scared but very dressy as I walked up the steps of the federal courthouse in New Orleans.

I don't recall meeting federal prosecutor Al Winters prior to the morning of the day I was scheduled to testify. But I certainly do remember being ushered into his big, beautifully decorated office that day, looking out the window at downtown New Orleans and thinking what a contrast this was to the St. Tammany DA's storefront cubbyholes off the alley behind the courthouse in Covington.

Mr. Winters briefly reviewed my testimony and explained what would be happening. This was a preliminary grand jury presentment. He would simply ask me to tell what happened to me on May 31 and June 1 and I would tell the jury my story. There would be no cross-examination today. He promised everything would be very routine.

Routine to him maybe. But I knew I was going to see Joseph Vaccaro and Robert Willie face-to-face again for the first time since they let me out of Tommy Holden's car just after dawn on that Sunday morning.

I also knew Robert Willie had been telling the authorities all summer that his case wasn't ever going to trial because there was no way I was ever going to testify against them. "Debbie said we could be friends. Everything was cool between us. She promised she wouldn't never talk against me. And she strikes me as the kinda gal who always keeps her word."

The investigators and I had a few laughs over that. But when I walked into that federal courtroom that day, I didn't feel like laughing at all. My knees felt all rubbery; my heart pounded.

I have no idea how long I was on the witness stand. It seemed like forever. I only glanced over at the defense table once, when I was asked to identify my kidnappers. Robert Willie grinned and winked at me, but I refused to make eye contact and carefully avoided looking in that direction again.

As many times as I'd recounted the kidnapping and rapes to police and prosecutors over the previous weeks and months, I had figured telling the story in court would be easy. It wasn't. Detailing what had been done to Mark and to me in a room full of strangers was harder and more embarrassing than I'd dreamed, made doubly so by the presence of the two men who'd done it. It felt like yet another violation of me just knowing that anyone in that courtroom had to only look over at Vaccaro and Willie to further visualize what they had done to me.

But I refused to break down. I stayed strong. I was "fine." I made it through my testimony and walked out of the courtroom feeling better and stronger than I had walking in.

My FBI agent friends congratulated me. "Hope that wasn't too difficult for you," Grover Leap worried. When the prosecutor came out a little later, he too told me, "Good job. Thanks, Debbie."

Evidently it was good enough. Even before I left the courthouse that afternoon we got the word: there would be no further federal court proceedings. Willie and Vaccaro had confessed to the kidnapping charges and would be sentenced to life in a federal penitentiary. The federal case was finished as quickly as that.

Mom and I walked out of the federal courthouse a little later with the FBI agents who would escort us home. We were all feeling relieved, satisfied, maybe even a bit like celebrating, knowing that our long and careful preparation had paid off so quickly.

I was tagging along behind while Mom walked a few paces ahead with Special Agent Grover Leap. I heard Agent Leap lower his voice a bit. Straining, I could heard him say to my mother, "You have an extraordinary daughter, Mrs. Cuevas. She's held up remarkably well through this ordeal. But I feel pretty confident in saying that all this is going to catch up with her someday. You'll need to watch her closely."

I couldn't make out what my mom said in response, but I remember saying to myself, *What is he talking about? He doesn't know me as well as he thinks. I've been strong this far. I'm fine! I really am.*

I'd almost convinced myself.

CHAPTER NINE

Public and Private Trials

Everything was not fine in my relationship with Mark. I continued to go over to his house every day. I drove him to physical therapy up in Covington, coaxing him to do five more leg lifts, to squeeze a rubber ball a few more times to strengthen his right arm, or to swim one more lap. It was harder to get him to work on his speech. Words came only haltingly, sounds muddled, syllables slurred together. Reading aloud, an important part of the therapy, proved especially laborious and discouraging for him.

The motivation and coaching I provided Mark relieved some of the guilt I harbored over the physical suffering he endured and I had escaped. But the daily responsibility I felt for keeping his spirits up weighed heavier and heavier—until I felt overwhelmed and trapped in a relationship that seemed totally redefined by the ordeal we'd been through.

We'd always talked a lot to each other before, but we no longer communicated. We couldn't do any of the fun outdoor stuff that had played such a big role in our relationship. Before, Mark had always been an active goer and doer; now getting him out of the house was a major challenge.

Despite the growing closeness of our relationship, we'd always maintained our own individual identities. We'd had different friends, different lives, and different worlds. Mark's injuries had suddenly changed all that. As his world had become smaller, it seemed as if he expected me to play a bigger and bigger part in it.

I knew how much he anticipated my daily visits—sitting and waiting impatiently for me for hours. Anytime I was later than expected, whether I'd been at the court house in Covington for some pretrial preparation or running family errands, Mark routinely acted put out with me.

Sometimes it felt as if his other friends only reinforced his frustration. They might stop by for an hour or so once or twice a week, but they'd always ask, "Where's Debbie?" It was like they thought I should be a permanent part of his life and wasn't meeting my obligations if I wasn't around every time they showed up.

I resented that attitude and felt even more trapped by their and Mark's expectations. But then that resentment made me feel more guilty, more obligated, more trapped.

My friend Kay continued to be the one oasis in my ever-widening desert of discouragement. We'd always enjoyed spending time at one another's houses and with each other's families. Kay relished the informal, laid-back, loosey-goosey approach to discipline my mom took; she actually seemed to enjoy the cramped togetherness required of four people living in one trailer. In contrast, I appreciated her family's structured lives just as much as I envied such trappings of affluence as a rec room furnished with a working jukebox and a refrigerator stocked with cases of soft drinks for visiting teenagers.

My mother and Kay had always liked each other, and they grew even closer that summer after the kidnapping. Looking back, I think it was because Mom worried so much about me that she came to rely on Kay as a sort of early warning system to help her gauge my emotional state.

Oddly enough, I think I grew closer than ever to Kay's folks during that same time period. They let me know I was welcome in the loving security of their home anytime. And they generously provided Kay the time and the encouragement she needed to be a caring presence in my life when I desperately needed that kind of friendship.

I approached the beginning of my junior year of school with feelings even more mixed than usual. After everything I'd been through, I looked forward to it as the first big step in my return to normality. But I also worried how my friends and classmates would react to the notoriety I'd achieved over the summer.

Turns out that in reality the results were mixed. It did indeed seem a relief to do something besides spending

time with prosecutors preparing their cases and helping
Mark with his therapy. But it wasn't as if the trial preparation really stopped, or Mark suddenly regained his
health. School merely added more demands to the heavy
load of responsibility I was already carrying.

The response of my classmates wasn't really better
or worse than I'd anticipated. There was a lot of whispering and pointing when I walked down the halls the
first few days of school.

"There she is. She's the one."

"Did you hear what happened to her during the
summer?"

I could pretty much ignore all that.

It was harder to take the awkwardness demonstrated
by some of my friends who either ignored or avoided me
because they suddenly didn't know how to react. Inter-
estingly enough, guys as a whole seemed to find it easier to acknowledge what had happened to me than did
many of my female friends. Many friends of my cousin
Jay Pennington and my brother, David, made a special
point of trying to make me feel welcome and affirmed
by saying things such as "Glad you're back, Debbie" or
"We're here if you need anything. Just let us know."

While it wasn't as if I was going to open up and
share my deepest fears and hurts with a bunch of high
school guys, I appreciated their protective attempts at
sensitivity and support. They seemed somehow more
comfortable around me than a lot of the girls I knew.

The two most responsive staff people were also
men. Mr. Ronnie Traylor, my honors chemistry teacher,
knew me from church. He made a special point to look
me up one of the first days to say, "If you need anything
Debbie, you know where my classroom is." He was the
one who helped me decide very early on that I was going
to have to miss so much time with the upcoming trials

that I probably wouldn't be able to handle the full load of honors courses for which I'd signed up.

Covington High's principal, Terry Bankston, also looked out for me. His son was one of David's best friends. He'd coached their Little League teams and had served as something of a father figure for my brother. Mr. Bankston wasn't just my principal, he was a family friend. He, along with Ronnie Traylor and the guidance counselor, worked out a half-day morning schedule. That got me the basic requirements needed to stay on track for graduation, yet left me the time I needed to prepare for the trials with the DAs or make up any work from morning classes I had to miss for a deposition, a court appearance, or whatever.

While the shortened schedule went a long way toward making my course load manageable, the downside came in my extracurricular activities and social life. Neither the cheerleading squad (which I'd been on in eighth and ninth grades) or the school dance team (which I performed with in tenth grade) were options that year. And my half-day schedule precluded my usual and regular involvement in things like Covington High's student council, the yearbook staff, or the honors society. Since I left school before lunchtime each day and couldn't hang around socializing after school either, I had almost no time at all for interacting with friends.

I'd spent much of the summer looking forward to a return to the school year's familiar routine, only to discover the beginning of my junior year seemed anything but routine. It wasn't just that my classmates looked at me differently; I felt different. Even my schedule was different. It distressed me to realize that the nightmare I'd endured at the hands of Robert Willie and Joseph Vaccaro impacted every corner of my life—that it had changed everything, even school.

If the routine of school couldn't seem "normal," I wondered if *anything* would ever again.

Things were quickly going from bad to worse between Mark and me. Even the time required by my part-time class schedule drastically cut the number of hours I could devote to him.

I recognized Mark's growing loneliness and frustration when I couldn't be with him; it wasn't like he tried to hide his emotions. His loneliness made me feel more guilty, and in turn more resentful. And then even more guilty.

I knew Mark didn't understand those emotions or my own frustration over things at school. And long talks aren't very productive when one person struggles to get out a few words at a time. I didn't know how to make him understand.

Things came to a head just a couple of weekends after school started. I'd gone with some of my friends to a meet-the-candidate barbecue for a classmate's father who was running for local political office. It was like a big community-wide picnic at Covington's Bogue Falaya Park.

Partway through the evening Mark showed up. I spotted him working his way slowly through the crowd, limping severely and walking unsteadily over the uneven ground. I hurried over to greet him and express my surprise. I think it was the first time he'd gone out anywhere since the kidnapping with anyone but his family or me. He said he'd come with some of his buddies and I immediately suspected they'd been drinking—his speech was harder than ever to understand. But clearly he was angry that I'd chosen to come to the barbecue with my friends instead of with him. And that my friends and I had been laughing and talking with a bunch of boys we knew.

Mark's uncharacteristic belligerence really scared me. I told him I didn't think his friends were doing him any favors and that he had no business drinking in his condition. The whole angry scene made me feel uncomfortable.

"I'm gonna leave and go home," I told him, "and I think you should too." When I turned and walked to my car, Mark followed me, angry that I wouldn't stay.

I got home that night really upset. And scared, for Mark and for me. Mark was like a swimmer caught in a powerful undertow that threatened to pull him under emotionally as well as physically. As desperately as I wanted to rescue him, to help pull him back, I was beginning to realize I wasn't strong enough. The longer this went on, the more of that undertow I experienced myself. Emotionally, I was drowning. And the sensation panicked me.

I walked over to Mark's house the next day. He was sitting in a lawn chair on his driveway, so I pulled another lawn chair out of the carport to sit beside him. I told him I'd made a decision. I swallowed hard and then managed to choke out the words: "It doesn't seem like anybody else realizes how much I was hurt because I don't have scars like yours. But I am hurt. And I don't feel like I'm getting any better.

"So I can't go on like this. I can't keep coming over here to sit for hours every day. I can't deal with all the responsibility of helping you, encouraging you, doing your therapy. I've got to find a way to get things back to normal at school. I need to get my own life back. And I can't be here all day, every day, and do that."

Mark stared straight ahead without responding.

"So I've decided I'm not going to be coming over for a while."

Nothing. Not a word.

"Do you understand what I'm saying? Why I have to do this?"

"Yeah." But he still didn't look at me.

"Mark, I'm sorry. I just have to do this. But I don't want you to use this as an excuse to quit doing your therapy." While I'd come to the conclusion that I could no longer help him, I didn't want to hurt him like this. "Okay?" I pressed.

"Just go!" he finally replied, his voice even and cold.

"Mark, I . . ."

"GO!"

So I stood up, feeling sick over what I'd just done, not knowing for sure how much Mark really understood. I walked to the house and into the kitchen to try to explain to his mom. In some ways that was harder than talking with Mark because Mary Brewster had been so open with me about how much she worried for her son. While she seemed to be coping very well with the challenge of Mark's slow, but steady physical recovery, the entire family really struggled to know how to respond to Mark's emotional reactions. All summer they'd let me know how much they counted on me to help keep Mark's spirits up.

And now here I stood in her kitchen telling Mary Brewster I could no longer help their son. "I just can't do it anymore," I said, my voice cracking. "I can't even take care of myself. I need a break."

Mary said she understood. But I knew she felt hurt. And scared. She had to be worried about how Mark would take this.

I said I'd told Mark, but I wasn't sure how much he really understood. I asked his mom if she would try to explain it to him. She said she'd do that.

I walked back home that evening feeling incredibly selfish and guiltier than I ever remembered feeling in my entire life.

In the days and weeks that followed I kept telling myself what I believed was true: *You didn't have a choice. You were in danger of drowning yourself.* But that didn't ease the guilt I felt about wanting to move on. What made all that even worse was knowing there were people who felt I was cruelly abandoning Mark in his moment of need.

And when I'd lie awake at night, staring at the ceiling, unable to sleep, I'd beat myself up wondering if those critics were right. Due in part to the guilt I felt, but also because of my own parents' history, I agonized over the question, *Will I ever be able to really commit to any relationship? Or will I always bail out the first time the going gets rough?*

I determined not to let the police and the prosecutors down as they finalized plans for the upcoming trials. I could do that much for Mark. And for Faith Hathaway.

The next step in the pursuit for justice was the murder trial. Since Willie and Vaccaro, in separate confessions, each accused the other of actually killing Faith Hathaway, a judge ruled they couldn't be tried together. Plans were made for simultaneous trials to take place in the Washington Parish courthouse up in Franklinton in mid-October. Willie would be tried in a basement courtroom at the very same time Joe Vaccaro was in court on the main floor.

Unlike my federal grand jury appearance in New Orleans, these were public proceedings. Spectators packed both courtrooms every day of the trials to observe the most sensational murder trial anyone in those parts could ever recall.

Because I'd heard both men refer to their "last girlfriend" and had also heard Joe Vaccaro graphically describe a murder scene that perfectly matched the

Hathaway case, the prosecutors put me on their list as a "sequestered witness." I wasn't isolated in some hotel room like a sequestered jury might be; I could actually sleep in my own bed at night. But it meant once the trial started, I wasn't allowed to talk to anyone about the trial, to go out in public where people might recognize or try to talk to me, to read newspaper accounts, or to watch television coverage about the trial. Neither was I permitted to observe the trial itself or hear any of the courtroom testimony presented before mine. I could only sit alone each day of the trial in a little courthouse conference room, reading or trying to keep up with my schoolwork as I waited to be called to the witness stand.

I dreaded facing my attackers again, especially after the way Robert Willie had behaved while I testified in New Orleans. And after I heard about the stunt Willie pulled the first day of the trial in Franklinton, I dreaded walking into court more than ever. Since Mark had no testimony to give in the Hathaway murder case, he was free to attend the trial. On that first day of the trial, when Robert Willie had looked back from his seat at the defense table and seen Mark limp slowly into the courtroom, Willie had mockingly drawn his fingers in a cutting motion across his neck and grinned at Mark. The assistant DA, Herb Alexander, and his investigator, Mike Varnado, who told me about the incident, were furious.

I found myself wishing, as I had several times before, that my kidnappers had resisted arrest and been killed by the cops who'd caught them in Arkansas. They deserved to die. The DA was seeking the death penalty in the Hathaway case anyway. If they'd just been killed in a shootout with the police, I'd have been spared the added ordeal of testifying in court, and it would have saved Washington and St. Tammany Parishes the cost of preparing and pursuing a capital punishment verdict.

There were two additional reasons I dreaded testifying in this murder case. The first was its lousy timing. The trial was slated to begin a little over a week before Covington High's homecoming. The football team had elected me as a junior class representative on the homecoming court. But if I was still a sequestered witness when the time came, I wouldn't be allowed to even participate in homecoming.

An even bigger problem, as far as I was concerned, was the awkward limitation placed on my testimony. The prosecutors needed me to tell everything I'd heard my kidnappers say relating to Faith Hathaway's murder. But since this trial was only for that crime, I was carefully and repeatedly instructed to make no reference at this time to my own kidnapping and rape. While the state planned to pursue those charges in a separate trial, it was ruled that any mention of those crimes here might prejudice the Hathaway murder jury and create grounds for an appeal. Or maybe even trigger a mistrial.

While I understood the legal rationale as the lawyers explained it to me, I resented the personal implications of what they were asking me to do. I was going into open court to tell a jury (not to mention all those spectators) what I'd heard Willie and Vaccaro say, but I wasn't going to be able to explain what I'd been doing in the company of two such disgusting, despicable characters. What were people going to think? That I'd simply been riding around with two murderers capable of such a horrifying crime? *How humiliating that is going to be!*

And it was.

The prosecutors had coached me to try to make eye contact with the jury when I testified. "We want them to connect with you," they said, "so they believe what you're saying."

I tried. But what *I* wanted was for those jurors, and everyone else in that courtroom, to believe what I couldn't say. *These creeps kidnapped and raped me. I wouldn't be caught dead riding around with the likes of them. Just being in the same courtroom with them like this is making me physically ill!*

I wasn't on the witness stand very long in either Willie's or Vaccaro's trial. And since their defense didn't want to risk the jury learning of the additional charges pending against their clients in my case, neither public defender bothered with much cross-examination.

It turned out that my humiliation over what the jury might think of me was nothing compared to the humiliation inflicted by Robert Willie himself. Before the jury was seated, he leered and grinned and winked and blew me kisses. I learned later that he'd discovered my mother's identity and when he saw her in court he'd smile and wave and say, "Hi, Mom." He'd even smirk at the Harvey's, Faith Hathaway's mother and stepfather. Such contemptuous behavior absolutely infuriated everyone related to the case—the prosecutors, the police, the families of all Robert Willie's victims.

I did eventually receive two small consolations after my testimony. During deliberations, when some members of the jury expressed confusion about the nature of my relationship to the accused and the murder, the judge himself decided to explain some of the circumstances. I felt somewhat vindicated by that.

The second consolation related to homecoming. Since my testimony was completed earlier in that week, Bill Alford and Herb Alexander, the two assistant DAs, petitioned the judge to allow me to take part. Just two days ahead of time, he ruled that I could.

On Thursday, the local paper ran pictures of Covington High School's entire homecoming court. The article identified me as one of the junior maids and said "Deborah Lynn Cuevas ... is the daughter of Mr. Tommy Cuevas and Mrs. Sharon Pennington of Madisonville. She is a member of the yearbook staff, the Beta Club, and is a former social studies fair winner, batgirl [for the varsity baseball team], and student council representative. She has served as a volunteer at the regional and state Special Olympic games. She enjoys camping and traveling. After graduation she plans on attending college."

That wasn't my only mention in the paper that week however. Most people knew I was also the unnamed "sixteen-year-old Madisonville girl" testifying in the sensational rape and murder trial making front-page headlines: "Willie, Vaccaro On Trial for Lives." Ironically, that page-one trial story was continued inside on the very page my homecoming court picture appeared.

I determined that even my personal connection with the lurid front-page stories about rape and murder would not spoil what I wanted to be a memorable night. And it didn't. In fact, homecoming turned out to be not only a blessed respite from the ongoing legal ordeal, but a meaningful family event. My brother, David, sophomore quarterback of the junior varsity team, dressed for varsity that night. My parents and grandparents cheered for him and for my cousin Jay, who was captain of the football team and who starred in the game itself. Poppie, dressed in his finest Sunday clothes, proudly escorted me across the field to be introduced to the fans at half-time. And then Jay and another senior football player presented me at the dance afterwards.

I even had a date to the homecoming dance. I'd wondered for a while if I would; guys weren't exactly lining up at my door to ask me out since I'd broken up with Mark. And I knew why.

I'd actually had one boy invite me to homecoming only to back out a few days later. I learned from a friend whose family knew his that the boy's mom, when she found out about his plans, had expressly forbidden him to go out with me because, she told him, "Everybody knows she's not a virgin anymore."

I ended up going with a casual friend I'd dated a couple of times. And we managed to have a good time in spite of everything.

I felt even better the following week when the juries returned their verdicts. Both men were convicted of murder (with less than forty minutes of deliberation in Willie's case). The same two juries were then asked to impose the death penalty.

Robert Willie's jury voted unanimously to sentence him to death in the electric chair. Joseph Vaccaro's jury couldn't agree to execute him; their deadlock meant he would receive life without parole.

Step two in this slow and complicated legal waltz had been completed. Step three, their trial for kidnapping Mark and me, and for my rape, was scheduled to begin the very next week at the St. Tammany Parish courthouse in Covington. But after all the headlines from the murder trial, and all the other pretrial publicity, Twenty-second Judicial District Judge Hillary J. Crain, who was to hear the case, granted a last-minute change of venue. The kidnapping/rape trial was moved to Baton Rouge—beginning now on November 10.

This decision meant even more missed classes for even more trial preparation. Plus all the travel back and forth to the state capital 75 miles away.

The lawyers warned me that this next trial was probably going to be the hardest for me. Mark still wasn't well enough to testify in court, so they were depending on me to recount all the details of the kidnapping and the three rapes.

Unlike the murder trial, where I merely testified as to what I'd heard them say about Faith Hathaway, this time I was going to have to publicly describe exactly what they had done to Mark and to me. This time the lawyers told me it was even more important that I look at the jury: "We need them to identify with you."

And unlike the federal grand jury testimony I'd given about the kidnapping, this time the defense attorneys would cross-examine me. "You'll do fine," the prosecutors assured me. "Just answer the questions you're asked. And don't offer any more in your answer than you are asked for."

The lawyers were right. For me this trial was the hardest of all.

I not only had to publicly recount in detail exactly what had been done to me, I had to repeat the filthy and disgusting language my attackers had used. I had to say words that had never before come out of my mouth. Which was why, despite the instructions given ahead of time, I spent most of my time on the stand staring down at my feet as I answered the lawyers' questions.

I managed a few times to force myself to make eye contact with the jury, and occasionally I'd glance up at the lawyers, but looking at the sea of faces out in that courtroom made it too painful, too humiliating to say what I had to say.

Robert Willie fed off my obvious discomfort. Having already been sentenced to death, he decided there was nothing more to lose; he would be as offensive as possible. Not only did he wave and wink and blow me kisses when I walked into court, he punctuated my testimony with his own obscene sound effects. When I was asked to describe the rapes, he licked his lips and made low, moaning "mmm-mmm" sounds, as if he was being sexually aroused by what I was saying. The judge got so angry he threatened to have a bailiff duct-tape his mouth shut if he didn't stop. I saw some members of the jury in tears as I struggled to finish my painful testimony.

The only way I could make it through was to try to think about it as if it was someone else's terrible story and I was simply the storyteller. Then I could spell out the facts without having to publicly process the feelings.

It worked. I made it through. And by the time I finished the jury was so clearly sympathetic that the defenders wouldn't have dared try a tough cross-examination—even if they'd wanted to.

After the second day of the trial, right after three FBI agents testified about the confessions they had taken from the defendants and the prosecutors had presented the majority of their case, Willie and Vaccaro surprised everyone by suddenly changing their plea to guilty. Willie laughingly admitted to his own lawyers that he planned to plead guilty all along, that he'd let the case go to trial in order to see me again and to force the state to spend as much money as possible. "They was trying to do it to us," Willie told the judge, "so we decided to make them spend as much as we could."

The judge was not amused. For the kidnappings, he gave each of them two life sentences to be served consecutively with their federal sentences. For the rape charges, he sentenced them each to another two life sentences scheduled to begin only after (and if) they completed those previous sentences. The judge made it clear in his sentencing that he had every intention of "warehousing" the two of them for the rest of their lives; they would never be candidates for probation or parole.

Assistant District Attorney Alford told reporters outside the courtroom he felt satisfied with the outcome. "The jury could not have done any more. We [meaning the state prosecutors] have gotten five life sentences for Vaccaro, plus four life sentences and one death penalty for Willie. Coupled with the three thirty-year concurrent federal sentences for kidnapping, these people should never walk the streets again."

There would, of course, be appeals. The death penalty, according to state law, required an automatic review by the State Supreme Court. Whether Robert Willie would ever be executed remained in doubt; there hadn't been an execution in Louisiana for almost twenty years. But all the authorities assured me, "They will never get out. Ever!"

Alabama still had attempted murder charges pending for what was done to Mark in that state, but they weren't likely to take that to trial. And Robert Willie's mother faced a January trial date for helping Willie and Vaccaro flee the state after she learned of the kidnapping and rape charges, but I wouldn't have to be part of that trial.

For me, the long and painful legal process was over.

On the way home from the courthouse in Baton Rouge, Bill Alford and Herb Alexander stopped with Mom and me at a Chinese restaurant in Hammond for a good-bye supper. It just so happened that the two defense lawyers were also eating there. Before they left, they came by our table to pay their respects. They told me they thought I'd been a "brave young woman." They said they were genuinely sorry that I'd had to go through the trials. They hoped I understood they had been appointed by the courts to represent Vaccaro and Willie. They were only doing their jobs.

I thanked them and said I did understand. They wished me well, said their good-byes, then picked up the check for our meals on their way out.

I got up and went to school the next day, but it took a little while for the truth to sink in.

No more trips to Covington. Or Franklinton. Or Baton Rouge. No more courtroom testimony. No more long days spent working in the DA's office on trial preparation.

I was actually going to miss my interaction with people like FBI Special Agent Grover Leap, Assistant DAs Herb Alexander and Bill Alford, and the DA's Investigator, Mike Varnado. But I knew they had to get on with their lives and careers. They had other criminals to pursue, other trials to prepare for. From my sixteen-year-old perspective, it seemed the end of that trial in Baton Rouge meant closure for them.

I was surprised that I didn't feel any closure of my own. I'd been expecting to. All through the trials I'd told myself, *Once this is over you can get on with your life.*

And that's clearly how everyone, including my family, expected me to feel. Now that the trials were finally over, we could all get back to life as normal.

I wanted that as much as anyone; I wanted it more than I'd ever wanted anything in my life. I did feel some satisfaction in knowing justice had been done. The legal system worked. The bad guys were going to be punished.

But I was just beginning to understand a difficult truth: Justice doesn't really heal all the wounds.

CHAPTER TEN

"Get On with Your Life"

I t's time you put this behind you and get on with your life."

That's the message I was getting from everyone who'd stood by me and been so supportive through the trials. The lawyers. My friends at school and church. Even my family. Some of them actually voiced such words. Others communicated just as clearly with their actions and attitudes, which let me know they were ready to put this behind them, to return to a normal routine, to get on with their lives.

I heard the message loud and clear, but it always seemed to trigger the same discouraged reaction from me: *Easy for them to say. Easy for them to do. They have the same lives to go back to. Mine has been changed forever. Shattered into a million pieces. Until I figure out how to fit all the fragments back together again, I don't have a life to "get on with." I don't even know where to start.*

There was no "normal" to go back to.

Many of my friends had tried to be supportive in the aftermath of the kidnapping and during the trials; they hadn't always known what to do or say, but they'd let me know they cared. While our interactions may not have been exactly "normal," I didn't expect them to be under the circumstances. And neither did my friends.

But now that the trials were over and my life seemed to settle back into a more familiar routine, those friends were ready to resume the old, "normal" and familiar patterns of our friendships. They tried to treat me like the same old Debbie. But that didn't work because I wasn't the same old Debbie. Because of this, not even my closest and most valued relationships felt familiar anymore.

Boys no longer seemed to know how to relate to me. I had been "just friends" with lots of guys, and I'd always had my share of dates. But now when I got asked out it was usually for some sort of "group date," as if guys didn't feel comfortable with me one-on-one. Boys I did go out alone with certainly didn't try to put any moves on me; they seemed more protective and less romantic. And while there were advantages to all of this, it was another reminder to me that everything had changed. My life wasn't normal.

The horrible ordeal I'd endured shattered my self-confidence, severely damaged my self-esteem, and left me feeling terribly vulnerable. But at least for those first few months the negative emotional impact of the ordeal had been countered by all the support, praise, and protection I'd received from so many sources. The authorities had needed my help, which had made me feel worthwhile. The humiliation of what I'd been through was offset somewhat by the recognition and praise I had received for my strength and courage. As bad as it felt to be viewed as the victim of rape and kidnapping, I was more than that—I was the star witness in headline-making trials, a central character in one of the most sensational crime stories ever in my part of the country. And even the sense of violation and vulnerability had been lessened for many months by the constant, protective presence of the law enforcement people I interacted with on an almost daily basis.

But now that the trials were over and everyone had decided it was time to get on with life, most of those positive, counter-balancing factors were simultaneously removed. All I was left with were the overwhelming negatives—insecurity, emotional pain, and vulnerability. Instead of life returning to normal, instead of things becoming better, everything was suddenly getting worse.

I remember my first panic attack. I'd gone to the hospital up in Covington to visit my grandfather. I stepped into an elevator and punched the button for an upper floor. A moment later, a man stepped in just as the doors began to close. Maybe thirty years of age, dressed like he'd just come from some blue-collar job, the man looked a little scruffy. As I felt the elevator lurch upward and I realized I was all alone with this stranger, panic struck. The elevator walls closed in. I could hardly breathe. I had to get out.

I hit the button marked "2" just in time to stop at the second floor. The instant the doors began to open, I slipped out into a busy hospital corridor, where I stopped and leaned against the wall until I could get my breath back and my heart quit pounding. I had never been a fearful person. The old me would have struck up a conversation with a stranger on an elevator and known half his life history by the time we got to the second floor. *What's wrong with me?*

The fear itself scared me.

After that, if I was alone in an elevator when a strange man got on, I'd pretend I'd forgotten something and step back off. Or I wouldn't take elevators at all.

I soon decided not to go anywhere alone if I could help it. If I went to the mall, I never seemed to get to or from my car in the parking lot fast enough. My heart would race. My legs would get all trembly. My hands would shake as I'd fumble to get the key in the lock.

Instead of getting better, the fear seemed to get steadily worse over time. More situations and more people scared me. First it was just men who looked unkempt, scruffy. Then it was guys with long hair. Then it was anyone who looked like he could be into the drug scene. Then it was any male stranger.

The way this was all progressing, I figured it wouldn't be long until I was going to be afraid of everyone and everything. I knew it didn't make sense, but I couldn't control the fears. I felt like I was going crazy.

Fear wasn't the only emotion that had the best of me. So did anger.

I was angry at my mom for a lot of reasons. I was angry that right about the time the trials ended she finally married the guy she'd been out with the night of the kidnapping. Mike was a diver who spent weeks at a time on deep sea oil rigs or working on other locations around the Gulf. I didn't think his hard-drinking, hard-living lifestyle was what my mom needed. I didn't like him. And when he moved into our trailer, I pretty much moved into my grandparents' house.

I resented the fact that Mom seemed so wrapped up in the excitement of her own life and her new marriage that she couldn't see how much I was hurting and that I desperately needed help. But when she expressed any concern for me, I resented that too. Particularly whenever she acted a little worried or protective, when she'd set some time limit on when I ought to be home, I resented the fact that she hadn't shown more concern earlier. *When it might have made a difference.*

I was also angry with God. During the aftermath of the kidnapping and throughout the trials, when I had convinced everyone that I was "fine," I actually felt grateful to God for the strength that enabled me to survive and feel okay. But now that things no longer felt "okay," I had lots of angry "why" questions. I felt like I'd gone out on a limb with my family when I'd made a personal commitment to God as a young teenager. Now his letting all this happen to me seemed like a real slap in the face.

The trials, and before that the preparation for the trials, had been such a major focus in my life that I'd drifted away from my friends at church over the summer and fall. During that same time period, the church youth leader who'd been such an important spiritual influence in my life moved away. There was no one who took any personal responsibility for me or showed any special interest, either by offering spiritual support or by keeping me connected to the youth group. I felt abandoned spiritually and was angry at God about that as well.

When I thought about it, I even got angry at the people who'd been most supportive over the past few months—the law enforcement authorities who'd befriended me and worked with me through the trials. I remembered the FBI agent's warning to my mother— to keep an eye on me because it was all going to hit me hard someday. *If they knew that all the trauma and feelings were going to surface like this, why didn't they try to do more to help me? If experience told them this is what was to be expected in cases like mine, why didn't they offer more help? I could use a little of that experience and understanding now.* But they were long gone.

I felt used by the system. And that made me angry.

As a result of all this anger, I lashed out. I couldn't reach God, and the authorities were gone, so the handiest targets of my anger were those closest to me.

I lashed out at my mom a lot. I let her know what a mess I thought she'd made of her life and mine. I even tried to put the blame for my kidnapping and rape on her for being such an inadequate mother that she hadn't been home to keep me from staying out so late. I condemned her new husband and what I thought was her irresponsible lifestyle. I said a lot of hurtful, judgmental things.

But I didn't limit my wrath to my mother. I dished out angry tongue-lashings to my little sister, Dionne. I called her stupid and criticized everything from her clothes to her character. I even hit her on more than one occasion. I launched verbal tirades at my brother and even snapped at my grandmother. Everyone felt the fallout from my anger.

It even affected my closest friendship. During the months of my limited involvement in school and church, Kay Bratton had developed new and deeper relationships with some other girls. Now, just when I was trying to get back in the swing of things, even my relationship with my best friend had changed.

While a part of me was happy to see Kay expand her social horizons, another part of me was jealous that she had been able to adjust and get along so well while my entire life had been on hold. I would never have admitted it, but I think that made me angry as well.

I think we both sensed a change. I would be irritable and impatient with Kay and critical in ways I never had been before. I don't even remember all the details now. But she and I disagreed about a boy she was dating at the time. When I gave her some advice that she ignored, I blew up at her. We argued. And neither of us would give in. So we went our separate ways. I missed her friendship more than I can put into words, but I was too angry to try to make up with her.

All this emotional turmoil eventually took a physical toll. When I began to lose weight and feel sick the spring of my junior year, my mom finally took me to a doctor who checked me into the hospital for a battery of tests.

After two days they had a diagnosis. They said I was anemic and suffering from acute depression.

"I'm not depressed," I insisted.

But Mom made an appointment with a counselor at a local mental health clinic anyway. When they found out I was the "sixteen-year old girl from Madisonville," they skipped the usual waiting period and gave me an immediate appointment. I told the therapist the same thing I told Mom: "I'm not depressed." But I did eventually admit the growing problem I had with my fears.

So we talked about that. She explained the difference between rational and irrational fears and then asked me to characterize mine. I quickly concluded they were, for the most part, irrational fears. Unfortunately, understanding that my fears were irrational didn't make them go away. Nor did it keep me from transferring those irrational fears to other "normal" situations.

When I was driving or riding in a car that stopped at a red light, I always had to check to make sure the doors were locked. If there was anyone standing at the curb or walking past on the sidewalk, I'd get especially jumpy. When I pulled into a parking spot, I had to get out of the car immediately. Just being in a car that wasn't moving made me feel vulnerable and edgy.

I know now that Mom was genuinely concerned about me, but I think that by the time the school year ended my family had put up with all the angry outbursts they could take. Both factors played a part in her suggestion, "It might be good for you to get away for a while, Debbie."

I was as tired of the constant conflict as everyone else, so when my mom proposed that I spend the summer with my aunt and uncle out in Texas, I was more than ready to consider the idea. "Uncle Tom could probably even give you a job," she said. That was enough to seal the deal for me.

I spent all but a couple weeks of that summer out in Huntsville, Texas, where my uncle managed the local Holiday Inn. I lived with Uncle Tom, Aunt Barbara, and their two young daughters and worked for Uncle Tom— hostessing or waitressing in the hotel restaurant, serving on the banquet crew, working the front desk, or filling in wherever he needed me.

I was my uncle's youngest employee. Most of the other part-time staff were college students from nearby Sam Houston State University. But I made a number of friends and fit right in with the crew despite the discrepancy in age. I found that I liked being part of an older crowd who didn't know my background and just accepted me for who I was without comparing me to the Debbie I used to be.

All in all, I think the summer away from home did some of what everyone hoped: It gave us all a much needed break from each other. Plus, it expanded my horizons while providing me a welcome new setting among people who, by seeing me as "normal," made me feel a little more that way.

The only real downside to my Texas experience came when I got back home and realized the contrast. An enjoyable summer spent working full-time hours and associating with older friends made me feel even more out of place when I started back into the high school routine.

I was a senior. For someone who'd been as involved as I was at the beginning of high school, this should have been a banner year. My friends were excited, ready to celebrate this milestone. In contrast, much of the high school scene now struck me as immature and unimportant. I'd lost my taste for high school life, and the effort it was going to take to get involved again just didn't seem worth it.

I enjoyed watching my brother, David, play during football season. But I missed my cousin Jay. He'd graduated in May as valedictorian, setting a standard I now realized I couldn't approach. I felt the Pennington family pride turning toward me as the next in line, and I knew I wasn't going to hold up well under such performance pressure.

What bothered me wasn't so much not being able to measure up to Jay; I never thought I could. The real problem was that I no longer even measured up to my own standards.

I took honors chemistry my senior year. I'd always taken honors courses before and had always done well. This time I struggled and quickly fell behind. Mr. Traylor, the teacher and fellow church member who'd been so understanding the year before, took me aside near the end of the first nine-week grading period.

"You're not making the grade in this class, Debbie," he said. "I know you've been under a lot of pressure, so I'll be glad to work with you. But I think you have a choice to make. You can try to hang in here with honors chemistry, or you could transfer out to a regular chemistry class. If you want to transfer, I can change the scheduling computer so the switch won't count against you on your permanent record."

I opted out of honors chemistry. What a relief that was. But for someone who'd spent her entire life being super-responsible and knocking herself out to live up to other peoples' expectations, it was also a bitter defeat. As far as I could remember, it was the first time in my life I'd ever quit anything. I'd never been a "quitter." Now I was.

Angry with myself, I wasn't getting along too well with my family either. Whenever Mom tried to be a mom and exert a little guidance or discipline, I'd explode at her. As far as I was concerned, any attempts at responsible parenting were too little, too late.

I'd tell her what I thought of her. Of her husband. Of her drinking. In no uncertain terms. And when she let me know just as clearly that I was making life miserable for everyone in the family, I knew she was right.

"I don't know why you're so unhappy," she told me, "and I don't know how to help you. But I think maybe you need to go back to church. You were happy back when you went to church."

"Quit telling me what to do!" I told her. "You don't know what I need!"

I'd been back to church from time to time. The trouble was that the anger I felt made me feel so guilty, so un-Christian, that I didn't feel as if I belonged there anymore. I was a failure spiritually.

And I wasn't doing too well academically either.

From the beginning of school I'd known that a big part of my second semester chemistry grade would depend on a science fair project of my own choosing. Research projects and exhibitions had always been a strong suit of mine; the big social studies project I'd done as a junior had won first place in both the local and regional competitions. But since I couldn't get excited about anything at school that senior year, I didn't even start thinking about the science fair until after Christmas.

In January, the Louisiana State Supreme Court ruled that there'd been something wrong with Robert Willie's death penalty sentence. When I learned they had ordered a new hearing, I didn't want to think about it. The lawyers assured my mom and my grandfather I didn't need to—that this was just a technicality, another required sidestep in this legal slow dance. They promised none of the legal maneuvering would need to involve me. So I tried hard not to think about it, which, of course, is never a very effective strategy.

Other kids were well into their science project research on topics of regional interest such as the oil industry, shrimping, and wetlands management. The day came and went when we were supposed to get our teacher's approval of a topic and I didn't have any idea what I was going to do. Other preliminary dates came and went. Other students had outlines and bibliographies okayed, yet I couldn't decide on a topic.

I spent time in the library thumbing through magazines and books, hoping something would leap off the page at me. Nothing did.

By that point, I was so far behind I doubted I could finish by the final deadline. I was spending more time trying to figure out how I could get out of the assignment than I'd spent actually working on it. But I hadn't come up with any legitimate out. It wasn't as if I could just get suddenly sick or something—we'd known about the assignment all year.

The only possible escape was to quit school. *That would get me out of everything.* But I quickly dismissed the idea as a little too extreme.

One day in February I was sitting in mythology class when I felt suddenly overwhelmed by everything. As the teacher lectured, I felt as if the entire room and my own body was closing in on me. My heart knotted tight in my chest. I felt like I was on the verge of throwing up.

I knew people were talking around me. But it was like they were all in a different world with some sort of sound barrier between us. They were there, but they weren't *really* there. Or maybe I was the one who was not really there.

I thought about the science fair. About the "F" I was going to get in science. And how I'd never gotten an "F" on anything in my life.

I looked around the room. I saw people I knew, but they couldn't see me. *They don't understand me! I don't understand me! Why is everything suddenly so hard? Why do I hate everything so much? What is happening here?*

Life is too short to live like this! I've got to get my life back! I'm gonna crack, I'm gonna lose my mind, if I have to sit here another minute!

I gathered my books together, stood up, and walked toward the door. The teacher stopped in the middle of her lecture and asked, "Where are you going, Debbie?"

"I've just got to leave," I said, as I continued out the door. *Let her think I'm sick and rushing for the bathroom.*

I went straight to the principal's office and asked the secretary what I needed to do to drop out of school. She looked at me funny, but she handed me a whole stack of "drop slips" I had to get signed by each of my teachers, the counselor's office, the librarian, a lunch-room lady, and I don't know who all else. I spent the better part of the next hour making the rounds, gathering signatures, turning in books, and cleaning out my locker. Since I had just turned eighteen, I didn't need any parental consent.

When I had everything in order, I headed back to the school office.

"Mr. Bankston is waiting to see you," the secretary said as I handed her the stack of signed forms.

I knocked on the door and walked into the principal's office. Mr. Bankston looked up from his desk and
asked, "What's this all about, Debbie? Why would you
want to drop out of school? Did something happen that
I need to know about?"

"No," I told him. "Nothing happened. I just don't feel
like I can go on. I feel like I'm about to have a nervous
breakdown or something."

He was quietly thoughtful. He knew what I'd been
through. "I tell you what," he said. "I'm not going to send
your withdrawal papers into the main office for a few
days. That way, if you change your mind, there will be
no problem with you coming back."

I thanked him but said I didn't think I'd change my
mind.

"Promise me one thing," he said. "Promise me you'll
go on to college."

"Oh, I'm still planning on going to college," I assured
him. "Those plans haven't changed."

"Good," he said. "I'm going to keep checking up on
you to make sure you keep that promise. I just wish
there was something I could do now, Debbie. If you
could tell me what was wrong, we'd try to fix it."

"But you can't fix me," I said as I turned and walked
out of his office.

CHAPTER ELEVEN

"You Can't Fix Me"

I didn't go home. I went right to Mom's work instead, to tell her I'd dropped out of school. She thought I was kidding. When I finally convinced her I wasn't, she still couldn't quite believe me.

"When did you decide to do this? How could you? What are you going to do now?"

"Today." "I didn't feel like I had any choice." And "I don't have any idea," were my answers. We were obviously going to continue this discussion later.

Next, I dropped by the shop where my grandmother worked and broke the news to her. Mimi was just as upset as my mother. Looking back, I guess it appeared on the surface like I must have been trying to get some sort of reaction. Subconsciously, maybe I was. But what I wanted most of all was understanding. I desperately wanted someone to realize how much I was hurting. How bad things were.

All I got were more questions. "Why in the world?"

"How can you do this now, two and a half months before your graduation?"

My grandfather took the news the calmest. "I know you've been through a lot," Poppie told me. "I just hope you can get back on track." But he also wondered, "What are you going to do now?"

"I don't know," I admitted.

But if I really was going to college, I needed a diploma. So I signed up for a GED class through a local adult education program. When I aced the pretest, the instructor assigned me to help tutor some of my class-mates. But he said I would still be required to complete the course before I could take the GED exam.

The second day of class I took a long look around the room at my classmates. There were some older adults for whom a diploma was either a blue-collar-job requirement or a matter of pride. And there were a few younger people, former dropouts who'd had just enough experience in the school of hard knocks to realize they couldn't get where they wanted to go in life without documented proof of a high-school level education.

I remember thinking, *Is this me? Is this who I've become?* It was depressing. So depressing I couldn't bring myself to go back for day three. I became a dropout from the dropouts.

Mom surprised me by quickly changing her tune from "How could you do this?" to "Maybe this is all for the best."

"Perhaps what you really need is to get away," she said. "To be out on your own for a while. Why don't you go back to Texas and get a job from your Uncle Tom again?"

I left in March in a yellow Opel my mom gave me to use. I began working in the Holiday Inn again and lived with my uncle and aunt for a few weeks, until I found a place of my own, rooming with a girl I'd met out there the summer before.

I returned home to Louisiana for a couple days in May—graduation time for my friends. I actually attended the Covington High School commencement exercises. Sitting in the stadium behind my old school, I watched the kids I'd grown up with walk out onto the field in their caps and gowns. Naturally, I had some regrets. I couldn't help wishing things had turned out differently. But I told myself, *You did what you had to do!* And I believed that.

After the ceremonies, several of my old friends invited me to their graduation parties. I thanked them and told them I couldn't go. I didn't tell them why, but the truth was that I was feeling too sad to watch anyone celebrate.

Some of my girlfriends even asked me to join them on a graduation trip to Florida. I had to tell them I couldn't do that either. As they headed for the beach, I started back to Texas, knowing I had a job to get back to. I had real-life responsibilities with rent and phone bills and car insurance to pay.

I still had my college plans, so I once again checked out the GED requirements. I learned that in Texas I could take the exam without any classroom instruction, and I passed with flying colors.

I figured I'd start at Sam Houston State University that coming fall. But then I learned I'd have to pay what seemed like astronomical out-of-state tuition until I'd lived in Texas over a year. There was no way I could afford that when I was barely paying my bills as it was. Plus, the admissions office told me it was too late to arrange for any financial aid or student loans for the upcoming school year.

If I was going to have to put my dreams on hold for a while to earn the money I needed to start college, I knew it made more sense to go back to Madisonville. I could live at home for free. Without having to pay rent, utilities, and a huge monthly long distance bill, I could actually save most of my paycheck. But running home again with my tail tucked between my legs would be one more failure. And I'd had enough failure lately. So I told myself, *I'm not gonna do that!*

I was eighteen now. The friends I worked with at the hotel were all older. When they got off work at night they often went out drinking. And I went with them.

At first, I'd just have a beer or two. Or, since we were in Texas, a couple of margaritas. Or beer and tequila.

I soon learned that drinking helped me forget my frequent feelings of failure. When I drank I didn't feel as fearful either. The responsibilities of life didn't feel so overwhelming. And the more I drank, the more all this was true.

I'd grown up seeing the negative effects alcohol had on both my parents, so I knew I needed to be careful. The first time I woke up with a hangover I told myself, *You've got to keep this under control, Debbie. You certainly don't want to drink too much.*

The trouble was deciding how much was too much. One drink was never a problem. Neither was two. Or usually three. After three, I had to be more cautious. I was always careful to ask myself, *Have I had too much yet? Am I okay so far?*

The bigger trouble was, of course, that with every drink, my definition of "okay" changed a little. My standards of measurement slipped. Invariably, I'd awaken the next morning knowing I'd drunk too much. That horrible realization always brought back memories of my parents' drinking and renewed determination to draw the line sooner the next time. I told myself, *It's just a matter of discipline and willpower.*

I remember the first morning I didn't remember. I woke up in my own bed, but I couldn't recall how I'd gotten there, or what had happened the night before. I knew I'd gone out with friends from work for the evening. We'd been drinking and dancing at some country-western club. I remembered that much. I also had a vague recollection of heading to someone's apartment for Tequila shooters after that. But I had no idea what time that was or what time it was now. . . . When I rolled over and looked at my bedside clock I remembered, *I have the early shift today!*

I started to jump out of bed; waves of nausea overwhelmed me. I staggered to the bathroom where a shower helped me feel a little more alive and a lot more sick. Somehow I managed to dress and shuffle out to the apartment parking lot.

My car was not there. When I realized I had no idea where it was, I felt a horrible sort of sickness that went way deeper than the worst physical symptoms. I was sick at heart and mind. I'd had an honest to goodness blackout. I'd suspected my father had had them. They'd always scared me. Having my own was absolutely terrifying!

What did I do? Where did I go last night? Who was I with? Each new question seemed more horrible than the last. *How am I going to get to work? Where is my car? What am I going to do?*

I walked back into my apartment trying to think. Since I didn't have a way to get to work, I didn't have any choice but to call in sick. So I did that; I lied to my Uncle Tom. Now I had to find my car. But how, without having to make the humiliating admission that I'd blacked out and didn't have a clue what happened?

Eventually, I decided to call the friend whose apartment was the last place I remembered being the night before. If I just said something vague about needing a ride to get my car maybe she'd say something that would let me know where it was—providing she knew. If our conversation didn't provide any clue, I'd use the same strategy and call every friend I'd been out with last night. Surely one of them would know what happened.

I lucked out on that very first call. Not only was my car at my friend's apartment, but she offered to come and give me a ride to pick it up. I don't think she suspected my blackout.

But I knew. And the experience shook me up so much I decided to go back to Louisiana in order to get out of the lifestyle I'd fallen into in Texas. Living at home again would mean swallowing my pride and accepting yet one more failure, but I was now so desperate and so scared by what was happening that I didn't see any alternative. I had to get my life back under control again. That was going to be easier to do in Madisonville than anywhere else.

Some positive things had happened during my six months absence from home. I'd missed the local headlines reporting on Robert Willie's new death penalty sentencing hearing. On June 29, 1982, yet another jury had sentenced him to be executed. One more step in the process everyone expected to take years to finish. If it ever was finished.

Of more immediate importance to my own personal life was my mom's changing marital status. She and Mike were on the verge of divorce. And while I was never sure how much was cause and how much effect, Mom finally began attending Alcoholics Anonymous. That determined first step toward change and a new lifestyle for Mom was pretty much the final straw for Mike. Complaining that she was no fun anymore, he left about the time Mom told him to get out.

I can't say I was a bit sorry to see him go.

With Mom herself now in AA, it was easier than I'd expected for me to quit drinking and change my own lifestyle. With Mike out of the picture and one less issue for the two of us to argue about, Mom and I began to rebuild and repair what had become a very strained mother-daughter relationship. We even took a couple evening classes together that fall, at a business school across the lake in New Orleans, in order to improve our secretarial skills.

One of my first weekends back in town I ran into Mark Brewster down on the riverfront. We talked for a while. He told me he was in a vocational rehab program, still trying to regain some of his fine-motor skills. I was pleased to note that his physical injuries were no longer obvious. He admitted he hadn't regained full strength on his right side, but he walked fine and his speech had really progressed. From time to time I noticed he substituted one initial consonant for another—he might say "cat" when he meant "bat." And I knew him well enough to realize he was a bit deliberate in organizing his thoughts before he spoke. But if I hadn't known what had happened or where he'd been, I might not have noticed anything outside the ordinary. He seemed in good spirits. He even told me he had recently begun a new dating relationship (with a girl he eventually married).

I was encouraged by our encounter. It made me feel less guilty to think, *Good! Mark is getting on with his life!*

Not too long after I returned from Texas I'd landed a job as secretary/receptionist/office manager for a shop that specialized in high-performance and vintage auto repair. My boss, Byrne Lobdell, was the husband of a woman who had long been my first and best adult friend. I'd walked up and introduced myself to Mary Pratt Lobdell on the school playground when I was in fifth grade. She told me right then that she was a remedial reading specialist—which is why I didn't know her. It wasn't until later that she told me how charmed she was to meet such a confident and sassy young girl. I liked her right away too. And it wasn't long until I developed a regular habit of dropping by her room before and after school just to chat.

By the time I started junior high, I was the regular babysitter for Mrs. Lobdell's two young children, and she was asking me to call her by her given name, Mary Pratt. During my early teen years, I'd go on vacations with the Lobdells and help take care of the kids. We developed such a close and trusting relationship that during my high school days they would let me borrow their cars. Byrne and Mary Pratt Lobdell had practically adopted me into their extended family.

Now, coming back from Texas and finding a full-time job working for Byrne Lobdell was a true blessing. He wasn't just a boss, he was a concerned friend. As Mary Pratt told me when they offered me the job, "We've been worried about you, Debbie. It's going to be good having you back where I can keep an eye on you and make sure you're okay."

For someone longing for a return to normality, someone seriously concerned about getting her life straightened out, that meant added but welcome accountability. I knew I needed that.

Another important step in my return to normality took place early in 1983 when I met Chris Blossman. Since I'd actually dated his oldest brother a couple of times before Trey took off on an extended trip to the Caribbean, Chris and I began our relationship rather slowly, as casual friends. But we soon hit it off so well that we started going out on real dates.

Very quickly I was viewing my relationship with Chris Blossman as a critical milestone in my life. Not only was this the most serious relationship I'd ever had, it was an obvious turning point in my recovery from the emotional trauma I'd been through over the past two and a half years.

What Robert Willie and Joseph Vaccaro did to me had seriously damaged my sense of self-worth. I could tell myself I was the same person I'd always been—the rational part of me knew that and could almost believe it—but I didn't *feel* the same.

I had felt so violated that I really, truly doubted any decent guy could ever love me unconditionally. I worried that anyone who learned what had happened to me, especially if he ever saw the pictures of Willie and Vaccaro, would be so repulsed that he'd never be able to look at me without thinking about what they had done. Not only would it be impossible to find someone who'd find me romantically appealing, I'd be lucky to find any respectable person willing to be seen with me in public.

My relationship with Chris Blossman quickly dispelled all those worries. I couldn't believe my good fortune. Chris was not only good-looking enough to have done a little modeling, he was a genuinely kind, thoughtful, and loving person who quickly let me know that he accepted and soon loved me for who I was.

Who Chris was didn't hurt my self-esteem either. The Blossman's were among the most prestigious and well-to-do families in St. Tammany Parish. Devout, church-going Catholics, his parents were highly respected throughout the community. Indeed, the Blossmans set the social standards around the North Shore. Their instant acceptance of me and their open-armed welcome into their family made me feel truly acceptable again. Their ready and willing inclusion of me in the life of their large, close-knit, and active clan (Chris was one of six brothers) provided me the benefits of yet another surrogate family. The Blossman's generosity of time, affection, and money, along with such trappings of wealth as a huge home on a family estate on the Tchefuncte River, a fifty-foot Gulfstar sailboat, and a vacation home in Florida suggested a measure of financial security and a world of experiences I'd never imagined in my life.

Chris and his family loved me. I could hardly believe it.

And my family loved Chris. Even my grandfather. Which was just as important to me.

As it turned out, I needed all the security I could get from my improved family relations, my new job working for an old friend, and my exciting new relationship with Chris Blossman. Because Robert Willie was back in the news again.

Since his convictions in my case, Willie had confessed to the 1978 drowning death of a Missouri man in a scuffle over drugs. Now he had confessed to the 1979 robbery during which St. Tammany Parish Deputy Sergeant Louis Wagner Jr. was shot and killed by one of the other participants. Because of this confession, Willie had been transported from the federal prison up in Marion, Illinois, back to Covington, for further questioning by Assistant DA Bill Alford. No one warned me he was coming. My grandfather just saw it in the paper.

It terrified me to know he was that close. For good reason. Back during the original trials we'd learned that Willie had escaped from the Covington Jail once a couple years earlier. What happened before could happen again!

I also knew what he'd said he would do if he ever did get out. During the trials, one of his former cell mates reported that Robert Willie had been so angered by what he viewed as my betrayal of him that he vowed if he ever escaped again, he would slice me up into so many little pieces my own mother wouldn't recognize me.

So I didn't sleep very well knowing he was back in Covington—less than five miles away. In August of 1983, I refused to follow the regular newspaper accounts of his trial and conviction for the second-degree murder of Sergeant Wagner. Yet with this new trial and its ongoing hearings, motions, and appeals, I never knew when I would pick up a local paper and see Robert Willie's picture staring back at me.

Robert Willie had been arrested thirty times before the age of twenty-one. How many crimes had he really committed? He'd admitted involvement in three murders. How many others had he killed? He was not the kind of man you wanted hating you.

I tried not to think about Robert Willie at all. But still the nightmares and the fear returned—with renewed intensity.

All the local trial publicity that summer helped convince me I'd made the right decision planning to enroll in Louisiana State University for the fall. After a year and a half out in the working world, I felt more than ready to jump back into the academic scene.

LSU was the most logical choice for me. I couldn't afford anything but a state university. Southeast

Louisiana University would have been closer—only twenty minutes from home—but too many of my high school friends went there. I needed to get farther away, to go somewhere people wouldn't know me as the "sixteen-year-old girl from Madisonville."

LSU was in Baton Rouge, 75 miles distant. That was close enough to come home whenever I wanted, but far enough to force me to live in a dorm and participate fully in campus life. Between my savings and student loans, I figured I had enough to cover my first year's expenses.

Chris, who was a year younger than I was, but two years behind me in school, planned to graduate from high school after the first semester and follow me to LSU. In the meantime, I returned to Madisonville almost every weekend to see him. On those Saturdays when the LSU Tigers played at home, Chris and I boarded the bus the Blossman family always rented for relatives and friends and rode back to Baton Rouge to experience big-time college football with an entourage of very enthusiastic, very serious, and very loyal fans. Not only was it fun, but it made for a memorable introduction to college life.

I enjoyed almost everything about my new college experience. Where some freshmen undoubtably felt lost among tens of thousands of students on such a sprawling campus, I relished the anonymity. And since I had nothing to concentrate on all week except my studies, I made excellent grades that first semester.

Things weren't perfect. I was terrified to walk across campus alone at night. If I was studying alone in the library I always made sure to leave and head back to my dorm before dark. And while guys weren't allowed to visit in girls' rooms, I still routinely avoided using the dorm elevators, especially at night.

Robert Willie was making headlines again. In response to emotional appeals from Faith Hathaway's parents, President Ronald Reagan signed an unprecedented executive order in November of 1983. He released Willie from federal custody, where he was serving three thirty-year sentences, so that he could be returned to the State of Louisiana for eventual execution. This development, which was another of those out-of-the-blue announcements, resurrected more old emotions.

Yet all in all, I was beginning to feel a sense of progress, as if things at long last were looking up again for Debbie Cuevas. It had taken me more than three years to get to this point, but I finally felt as if I could begin to do what people had been telling me I needed to do for so long. Starting college was obviously an important step. *Maybe, just maybe,* I thought, *I am now ready to get on with my life.*

The following year dispelled that thought.

CHAPTER TWELVE

The Nun and the Execution

Growing up, I often imagined myself becoming a teacher. But when I learned what educators were paid in Louisiana, I thought, *No way am I going to invest in four or five years of college just to take a job that pays only $18,000 a year.* So I started college not knowing what I planned to do.

Accounting had seemed like a good option until I took an Intro to Economics course my freshman year. I quickly decided that life is too short to take the three more economics courses required for an accounting degree.

I had thoroughly enjoyed the Intro to Criminal Justice course I also took as an elective my first year, but career options for women in criminal justice seemed fairly limited. Parole officer was the most common, but they got paid even less than teachers. And while I thought the job of FBI agent would be an interesting challenge, I learned only a very tiny percentage of applicants ever got accepted at the Bureau's academy. And if I did happen to make it, the danger, travel, and long hours required of agents didn't seem conducive to motherhood or the kind of family life I'd always envisioned.

I thought Geology 101 was fascinating. However, by the time I took a second course in that subject, I decided I much preferred social science to physical science. That and the fact that it was the fall of 1984—a presidential election year—made me think a course in political science might prove to be an unusually relevant and timely experience the first semester of my sophomore year. Little did I know ...

The electrocution of Patrick Sonnier in the spring of 1984, only the second execution in Louisiana after a twenty-two year moratorium, had stirred up the death penalty debate around the state. What little I heard about Sonnier's story at the time had seemed to confirm everything I'd been told: these cases took years to wind their way through the courts. Sonnier had been on death row at Angola for six years before his sentence was carried out.

Robert Willie had been at Angola only a few months, so I was surprised that fall when Willie's case moved onto the fast track and created further interest in the death penalty debate among the media and, of course, on college campuses. I remember the day in my political science class when one outspoken coed announced she was against capital punishment because "Killing is wrong, no matter what the circumstances!"

She seemed so sure of herself, her reasoning so simplistic, that I spoke up before I could check myself. "Have you ever been the victim of a violent crime? If you had, you wouldn't be so sure there's only one reasonable position."

Angered by my response, my classmate snapped back, "And when was the last time you were the victim of a violent crime?"

"It was in 1980," I told her matter-of-factly. "I'll give you details later if you want. But let me tell you right now that personal experience with violent crime gives victims and their families a very different perspective!"

That wasn't the only such discussion I found myself a part of during my sophomore year. I joined the Kappa Kappa Gamma sorority that fall and overheard a lot of talk around the sorority house. I never had much patience for anyone who adamantly declared, "I'm against capital punishment under any circumstances!"

I always wanted to say, and sometimes I did, "When was the last time you had a family member kidnapped, dragged into the woods, raped, and mutilated beyond recognition?" I was thinking particularly of Faith Hathaway's parents. "If that happened to someone you loved, do you think you'd still be so opposed to the execution of the person who did it?"

Believe it or not, sometimes I would play devil's advocate on the other side of the issue. It also upset me to hear people make sweeping statements such as, "We should fry 'em all as far as I'm concerned! Anyone on death row deserves to die! Their victims died; they should too!"

To that I might say, "Do you know what you're saying? It's easy to make snap judgments and sweeping condemnations when you see it as only a theoretical question. But there are real people involved. When you realize that, you know it's not a question you can take so lightly. It's a real tragedy."

I think what bothered me in all the talk, all the debate, was people taking either position without any real thought—people not considering the real issues. I wanted everyone to wrestle with the questions on the same level I did, though I knew they couldn't.

I was deeply conflicted. And the farther Robert Willie's case went, the more conflict I felt. I knew better than almost anyone what kind of evil he'd done, but I'd also seen enough of him that I couldn't view him as some theoretical, faceless monster. He was a human being. That meant he had been created in the image of God, so there had to be a part of him that wasn't all bad. He had once been someone's little boy. It was just that somewhere something had gone wrong.

I realized all that, yet at the same time I wanted him dead and gone so I could feel safe again. So I wouldn't have to be so afraid to walk alone at night or too scared to get on an elevator. So my own horrible ordeal would finally be over. So I could finally get on with my life.

But were those things really worth someone dying for? Was it right to wish someone dead because I thought it would make my life better or easier?

Sometimes I asked myself, *Does Robert Willie deserve to die for what he did to me?* Then I felt guilty about even asking that question, knowing that other people actually died, or had their child die. *What Robert Willie did to me was nothing compared to what he did to Faith Hathaway or even to Mark. So who am I to debate his punishment in my mind? I shouldn't have that right.*

Then I'd end up feeling guilty.

I felt conflict about almost everything related to the case, which is why I tried so hard not to think about it. I studiously avoided both the morning papers and the evening news. I knew I could rely on my family to keep me informed about what I needed to know. Poppie, in particular, walked a fine line between protecting me from what he thought I didn't need to hear and preparing me for any new developments he worried might upset me if I did find out.

I remember Poppie telling me about news reports saying "some nun" had been chosen to serve as Robert Willie's "spiritual advisor." I wasn't sure exactly what that meant or how I felt about it. Part of me thought, *He certainly needs a spiritual advisor.* On the other hand, *Why bother?* And yet another part of me resented it: *No one is offering me a spiritual advisor, and I could sure use one right now!*

Near the end of October my family called to warn me there was going to be extra publicity about an anti-death-penalty march from New Orleans to the steps of the state capitol in Baton Rouge. The nun who was Robert Willie's spiritual advisor, Sister Helen Prejean, had made the papers and all the newscasts as a spokesperson for the group.

I remember thinking, *What business does this woman, a total stranger, have stepping into the picture at this point? She's a nun, for crying out loud! What does she know about the real world?*

Despite having spent my early years in the Catholic church, my image of nuns was colored by limited personal experience. My great-uncle Johnny, who was married to Mimi's sister, had a biological sister who had become a nun. From time to time when I was little, Uncle Johnny would take me out to the convent to visit her. All I really remember about her was that she worked in the convent kitchen and baked wonderful cinnamon rolls, which she shared with me before she sent me out to the duck pond with stale crusts of bread to feed the

geese. She spent her entire life in that convent with little or no exposure to the outside world.

*What business would a person like that have work-
ing with criminals on death row? Surely this Sister Helen
Prejean could have found someone more suitable to min-
ister to, someone more deserving of her help than Robert
Willie.*

But to be perfectly honest, what bothered me most
about this nun's involvement was the extra publicity she
seemed to be generating. Things had been pretty quiet
since I'd been at school. I'd maintained a pretty low pro-
file myself. Now suddenly Sister Helen Prejean and her
fellow protesters were stirring up added interest in and
scrutiny of Robert Willie's case. My case.

I worried that if some of the protesters learned my
identity and my whereabouts, they might try to confront
me about the role I had played in Robert Willie's conviction and sentence. And what if his family and friends
learned where I was? I was particularly afraid of his
mother. She'd helped him escape after the kidnapping,
perjured herself in court, and then spent six months
in jail herself. As angry as Willie was with me, as often
as he'd threatened me, I didn't know what his family
might do to anyone they might blame for his conviction.
I just wished Sister Helen Prejean would quietly stick to
her "spiritual advising" and quit stirring up attention
with any more protests.

But she didn't.

She made more headlines when she testified on
Robert Willie's behalf at the November parole board
hearings held at Angola State Prison. And after the
parole board turned down the appeal and voted to carry
out Willie's death sentence, she continued to question
the morality of the state imposing the death penalty
on anyone.

By this time most of my family and friends (along with a majority of the population of Madisonville) were nearly as ready to condemn Sister Prejean as they were Robert Willie. I heard lots of people derisively question the value of "spiritual advisors" for death row inmates. "Animals like that don't deserve any last minute chance to make their peace with God. He might say he's changed, but who's gonna believe it? That nun is just wastin' her time!"

While I didn't agree with that theory—I felt she had every right to be a spiritual advisor if that's what she felt God wanted her to do—I was still irritated by what I saw as her attempts to meddle in the legal process. I resented the extra attention she drew, especially when that attention seemed more focused on the well-being, the salvation, or whatever, of the convicted than on the forgotten victims. *Where was the help I needed when I felt so alone?*

On one level I was almost jealous of the concern Helen Prejean was demonstrating for Robert Willie. As if he was as much a victim as those people he killed.

When I learned Sister Helen had just recently contacted the Harveys, Faith Hathaway's parents, I felt annoyed that she hadn't ever bothered to contact Mark or me. Were we not considered victims, since we hadn't died or hadn't been sentenced to die?

I knew Sister Helen didn't owe me a personal explanation. But I kept wondering why she hadn't called to express concern, explain what she was doing, and why. *I would listen. At least I think I would.*

I was probably as troubled about Vernon and Elizabeth Harvey as I was about Helen Prejean. I felt terrible about their loss and the obvious pain they suffered as a result of their daughter's horrifying death. But from the first time I'd seen them with their psychic on my visit to Fricke's Cave with the law enforcement officials, the Harveys had made me extremely uncomfortable.

Before and during the trials the Harveys and I had numerous face-to-face encounters in lawyers' offices and around the courthouses. They always acted friendly and expressed genuine concern about how I was holding up to the pressures of the ordeal. But where I was constantly trying to control my emotions, the Harveys always seemed to expose theirs. Elizabeth couldn't ever talk about Faith without crying. Vernon was always angry. I tried to avoid any sort of emotional scene or confrontation; the Harveys didn't.

I remember standing in the courthouse hallway one day when I heard the elevator doors open right behind me. My mother gasped and then quickly grabbed my arm to practically drag me down the hall and out of the way. When I pulled loose and looked back to see what had happened, I spotted the back of Robert Willie's head in a ring of deputies leading him down the hall in the opposite direction. I felt immense gratitude to my mother for preventing an unwanted encounter.

In contrast, Vernon Harvey staked out any elevator or hallway where he thought Robert Willie might appear. I can't count the number of times I overheard him speculating on what routes the escorts might take. "They're gonna have to bring that _____ (he had a long list of horrible names he used for Vaccaro and Willie—especially Willie) through that door any minute. And when they do, I'm gonna be there. He's gonna see me. He's gonna know he's gotta pay for what he did. . . ."

Vernon Harvey took every opportunity he could find to get right in Robert Willie's face (or as close as he could come) and scream horrible, damning things at the man who had so brutally butchered his stepdaughter. Sometimes Robert Willie would simply grin as the deputies fought to pull Vernon away; more often than not he'd taunt Vernon by saying something ugly about Faith or he'd just scream his own curses back. One time the deputies found a revolver on Vernon. Another time he chased a sheriff's car transporting Willie all the way across the causeway to New Orleans. While I felt for Vernon's pain and never blamed him for his anger, I saw nothing good to be gained by his confrontational tactics.

At the end of the trials, when the murderers were both convicted, the Harveys went out of their way to express their gratitude to me, "For all you've done for us and all you did for Faith." It was as if they thought they owed the conviction of their daughter's killers to me— as if they felt I'd survived for the sole purpose of bringing justice, of seeing the men who were guilty punished.

I don't think they ever really viewed me as a substitute for their daughter. But in their minds, by sharing an experience with the same kidnappers, I shared some sort of bond with Faith. This meant they too felt some sort of bond with me, some connection they refused to let go of and very much wanted me to feel. This too made me uncomfortable.

From time to time in the months after the trials ended, Elizabeth Harvey would call, saying she'd been thinking about me and wondering how I was getting along. Mom usually took the calls, made excuses as to why I couldn't come to the phone, and would report that I was doing fine. But it was obvious Elizabeth was thinking about Faith and trying to make one more connection with her daughter through me.

The times I happened to answer the Harvey's calls were extremely awkward. Elizabeth would start by asking how I was doing, but almost before I could answer she'd be rambling about Faith, recounting yet again the details of her daughter's disappearance and death. "You know she was such a good girl. She was out saying goodbye to her friends that night because she was leaving to join the Army the very next day . . ."

Every time, as she talked about Faith, she would break down and begin to sob. And every time, above her sobs you could hear Vernon in the background, ranting and raving, "That SOB is going to fry!" among other things.

It got to where I never wanted to answer the phone. And when I did, as soon as Mom realized it was Elizabeth Harvey, she'd take the phone from me and try once again to explain that I couldn't keep talking about it. That I was trying to go on with my life.

Gradually the calls from the Harveys slacked off. Until some new development, some hearing, some appeal came along in the case. Then they would begin once more to call to "check on me."

Once Robert Willie was transferred back to Louisiana from federal prison and the death sentence became a public issue again, the Harveys began making regular appearances in the local news. They'd demonstrated and cheered outside the gates at Angola the night Patrick Sonnier had been executed. They'd even called my house a couple of times, asking if I'd like to go on some talk show with them to speak out in favor of the death penalty.

When Mom tried to explain I wasn't interested in doing that, Elizabeth told her, "We gotta do this for Faith. Faith needs us to do this. We're doing this for all the victims."

"Debbie doesn't see herself as a victim," Mom told her. "She's trying to get on with her life."

But Elizabeth Harvey could never stop viewing me as the sixteen-year old kidnapping and rape victim who'd testified against Faith's murderers. She couldn't stop seeing Faith as that "good girl who just went to say goodbye to her friends the day before she was going to join the Army." She wanted to somehow relate to her daughter, or at least her daughter's memory, through me.

Somewhere along the way the Harveys seemed to have exchanged their inconsolable grief for an all-consuming mission to "see justice done"—to deliver vengeance not just to their daughter's murderers but to everyone on death row. When Helen Prejean and the other marchers arrived on the capitol steps at the end of their anti-death-penalty march, the Harveys were there to proclaim their own position. They too attended the parole board hearing to talk about their daughter and tell why her killer deserved to die.

Anytime, anywhere, to anyone who would listen, the Harveys would speak out "on behalf of all victims" and in favor of the death penalty. Vernon especially provided many a memorable soundbite when he repeatedly vowed the day Robert Willie was executed "will be the happiest day of my life." He even promised the media he would celebrate the occasion by "dancing outside the gates of Angola."

Still, I was surprised by the call that came in the wake of the parole board hearing and the official setting of Robert Willie's execution date for December 28, 1984. Elizabeth Harvey phoned to ask Mom how she could reach me at school. She wanted to tell me how to go about applying to be a witness at the execution. She said she and Vernon wanted to be there to see Robert Willie die and she hoped I would, too.

Mom refused to give Elizabeth my campus phone number and told her not to attempt to reach me. She knew beyond a doubt I wasn't interested in attending an electrocution.

After she finally managed to get Elizabeth off the phone, Mom called me to tell me about the conversation. Not only was I shocked by the very suggestion, I couldn't believe the Harveys still thought I wanted to be part of their mission.

The Christmas spirit seemed strained that year. It was impossible to buy gifts, make plans, and look forward to celebrating the morning of December 25 without also thinking about what was scheduled for midnight three days afterwards.

For months, whenever I'd heard other people curse and complain about the tedious process of appeals and hearings that invariably delayed justice and sometimes dragged out capital punishment cases for years, I'd taken comfort in telling myself, *It's not going to happen soon. There will be yet another appeal. One more hearing. A last minute legal hitch. Or some other delay.*

But the wheels of justice ground steadily on.

As the holidays approached with no new developments I remember thinking, *Nothing's happening now, but when everyone goes back to work on the twenty-sixth or twenty-seventh, some judge is going to agree to hear an appeal or the governor's going to sign something at the last second. And this will spoil Christmas for no good reason at all.*

Part of me hoped that someone *would* intervene. Still, another part of me wanted Robert Willie to die in hopes I could regain some sense of safety and security. When that seemed cold-hearted and selfish, I told myself, *No one would want to live forever on death row anyway. What kind of life could that be? Execution is probably better. It will bring an end to everyone's pain and misery. And I'll feel safe again.*

The unspoken subject hung like a pall over everything. Christmas lights looked dimmer. Christmas carols sounded muted. Christmas cheer felt more subdued.

No one wanted to talk about it, least of all me. But a couple days before Christmas, Mom and Poppie sat me down to discuss our strategy if the execution plan continued as scheduled. We knew the local media would be looking for a reaction story. Since I was no longer a minor, they might not want to take no for an answer.

"You need to be out of town during the execution," Poppie and Mom said. I agreed. I'd get Chris to take me back to Baton Rouge. After celebrating Christmas Eve with my family at Mimi and Poppie's house, and Christmas day with the extended Blossman clan, I could hole up for a couple days in the condominium the Blossman's had bought Chris and his two brothers to live in while they attended school at LSU. It seemed like a good plan to me; no one would look for me there.

That is, if nothing happened to stop the execution.

Nothing did. Chris and I took off the morning of the twenty-seventh.

I didn't look at a paper all day. I avoided TV and radio as well. I'd been following the news coverage more closely at home over the holiday break. I'd listened to reports about the upcoming execution and to comments both pro and con—including quotes from Sister Helen Prejean, who was always identified as "Robert Willie's spiritual advisor."

I still had some of the same reservations about her involvement. But I was also finding new comfort in knowing that Willie had someone who would be with him right up to the end, someone who would give him every possible chance to make his peace, to experience a real, meaningful, personal encounter with God.

If this sounds like a noble wish, or a surprisingly saintly attitude on my part, I must admit it was also somewhat selfish. As much fear as I had of Robert Willie alive, as much as I knew he hated me and wanted revenge, I worried that I might have even more to fear from him dead.

It wasn't that I was superstitious or really believed in ghosts. But the thought of someone dying who hated me so much, of having such an angry, vengeful spirit being loosed into eternity had begun to trouble me. I'd only recently begun to cope with the reality of a living but incarcerated Robert Willie who hated me. How might his death affect my nightmares and all those irrational, but very real, fears? I didn't know. And that unpredictability frightened me.

I couldn't help thinking that if Robert Willie did experience some last-minute conversion, if I could hear that he finally expressed some remorse, that he quit hating me before he died, that he no longer vowed revenge, I might sleep a lot better at night and not be so afraid in the dark. Maybe I would even begin to feel like I could finally get on with my life.

I went to bed early that night and tried to sleep. Of course, I couldn't.

So I lay in the dark, staring up at the ceiling, and tried not to think about Robert Willie. I couldn't manage that either.

I thought back over all the days and months and years that I'd hated Robert Willie and everything about him. For who he was. For what he did. To me. To Mark. To Faith Hathaway.

I recalled the anger, the shame, the humiliation, the guilt, the stomach-turning repulsion that had all been part of that hatred. When I realized I hadn't felt the intensity of those old emotions for a while, I decided there was no point in harboring and holding on to a word—"hate"—to describe something I didn't really feel any longer.

Realizing I no longer "hated" Robert Willie freed me from some of the hold he'd had over me. If I didn't hate him, maybe I could actually forgive him. Not for his sake; he would never know. But for my sake. Maybe then I would be free to get on with my life.

That's what I needed to do. As much as I hated the thought of him dying hating me, I realized it might be just as bad for him to die with me hating him.

Could I truly forgive him? In a sense, I already had. I'd heard people say Robert Willie could die five times in the electric chair and it wouldn't be half the pain he deserved for what he'd done, but I didn't feel that way at all. Not anymore.

So yes, I could forgive Robert Willie. But I couldn't tell him. There was no one to tell—but God.

Lying there in bed in the dark, I began to pray. "Lord, please help me deal with whatever happens tonight. I really do forgive Robert Willie. As best I can anyway. If the execution goes on, please make it fast and painless. I don't want him to suffer anymore. If he dies tonight, help his death to heal the Harveys and their pain. Amen."

With that prayer pronouncing my forgiveness of Robert Willie, I gained an emotional release, a sense of freedom I don't know how to describe. Somehow it cut me loose from the control Robert Willie had over me for all those years. I fell asleep.

When I awakened the next morning, I was alone in an empty condo. Chris was gone. But he'd left the morning newspaper out for me to see.

I didn't bother to read past the headlines.

There had been no last-minute reprieve. No stay.

Robert Willie had been executed last night.

This morning Robert Willie was dead.

For a long time I couldn't decide how to feel. Mostly I was numb. I told myself, *It's over at last.* I certainly wanted it to be over.

At the same time, I think I'd finally realized that no punishment—not even the ultimate punishment, the ultimate justice—could ever heal all the wounds.

CHAPTER THIRTEEN

Still No Peace

Before Robert Willie's execution there had been some debate about where he would be buried. Many of his relatives were so appalled by the shame he'd brought on their family name that they didn't want him interred at the old, private, Willie family cemetery up near Folsom.

When it looked for a while like the authorities might have to request one of the nearby public cemeteries to donate an "indigent" plot, I'd asked Poppie if he thought Robert Willie might be buried in the Madisonville Cemetery. I was reassured when my grandfather said he didn't think so. I didn't want Robert Willie laid to rest in the same plot of land where my relatives had been buried for generations.

In the end, the Willies relented and agreed to bury him in their own graveyard. A Covington funeral home was chosen to handle all the funeral arrangements.

I didn't know what I was supposed to do in the wake of my rapist's execution. I knew I had forgiven him—to the best of my ability anyway. But the act of forgiveness seemed somehow incomplete and less than satisfying when there was no one to accept it, no one to acknowledge it or even know that it had been granted. I wondered if there was some way his family could accept on his behalf. What if I went to his funeral as sort of a symbolic gesture? Would that be appropriate? Emily Post had never addressed this scenario as far as I knew.

I'd pretty much dismissed the idea myself before I floated it past my grandfather. Poppie acted appalled at the mere suggestion of attending the funeral. "Absolutely not! It would *not* be appropriate!" he exclaimed in no uncertain terms. I knew in my heart he was right.

Still, I couldn't help wondering what had happened with Robert Willie at the end. Did he ever accept accountability for his actions? Had he even acknowledged what he had done? Had he made peace with God? Shown any sign of sorrow or remorse? Did he die still blaming my "betrayal" for his conviction?

I thought maybe if I could know those things, I could feel a stronger sense of closure. It took a long time for me to finally accept the fact that I would probably never have those questions answered. Yet in deciding to forgive Robert Willie as best I could, I had freed myself from any feelings of fault or responsibility for his execution. Neither was I haunted by any regrets of my own, nor by the fear of his vengeful spirit.

Almost five years after the kidnapping, I was ready for the central focus of my thoughts, my emotions, and my life, to shift away from the past and more toward the future. That began to happen through some important developments at LSU.

Even before the second semester resumed in mid-January of 1985, I received word there was a resident opening at the Kappa Kappa Gamma house. Among the new pledges, I was next in line if I wanted to live at the sorority. The decision was a no-brainer as far as I was concerned; room and board was actually less than I'd been paying to live in the dorm, and even though I now had an on-campus job working twenty hours a week in the Office of Student Aid and Scholarship, finances continued to be a serious consideration.

By any standards, my sorority was among the strongest organizations at the university. They had a fun-loving, though not wild, reputation. Academics were emphasized; Kappas had one of the best GPA averages among all the Greek chapters on campus. A lot of New Orleans girls belonged there; many, if not most, came from private schools and would have been considered well-to-do. There was strong alumni support, which helped keep the cost down. The house itself was a showcase—a huge, three-story, antebellum-style mansion on the shore of a campus lake. It was, far and away, the nicest place I had ever lived. Whenever I walked into the front foyer with it's big crystal chandelier, or strolled through the living room where an arrangement of flowers always sat atop the concert grand piano, and especially every morning when there were always two cooks waiting in the kitchen to take and prepare my personal breakfast order, I felt like I ought to pinch myself. I'd never lived so well—even in my dreams.

After nearly two years of academic uncertainty, I was just as excited about my course of study. That spring semester of 1985 I finally declared my major: special education.

I had always loved kids, and having been a volunteer worker for the Special Olympics since the ninth grade, I had developed a heart for underprivileged and disabled kids. I decided that the chance to pursue an emotionally rewarding career of service outweighed the drawbacks and concerns I had first had about inadequate pay. It also seemed to be a career that could fit into my plans to be a wife and mother.

Chris hadn't officially asked me to marry him, but we had reached a point in our relationship where I think we both just assumed we would have a future together. We even talked about marriage, both agreeing we wanted to finish school before we took that step.

Our deepening relationship provided the emotional underpinning required to help heal past wounds and lay an emotional foundation secure enough to begin building a future on. He was the only one with whom I shared my deepest feelings of embarrassment and shame about the kidnapping and rapes, about Robert Willie and Joseph Vaccaro. Many were the times I asked him, "Doesn't it ever bother you, like it bothers me, that family and friends have seen their pictures in the papers, realize what kind of people they are, and know exactly what they did to me? Do you ever think about that?"

"No," Chris told me. "Why would I? It was not your fault, Debbie. You had no control over what happened to you."

I always found a measure of welcome reassurance in those words.

Still, sometimes I found it hard to believe. There was enough residual insecurity that I frequently wondered, *How can he say it doesn't bother him, that he doesn't care or think about what they did to me? He's seen their pictures. How can he say it doesn't matter? It has to. He has to think about it.*

Yet he said he didn't. And I wanted to believe him, because I loved him. And because he loved me. Our relationship became my greatest hope for the future at a time when I still longed for closure on the past.

A lot of factors, a lot of people, made that closure difficult.

The death penalty issue certainly didn't go away. LSU's student activities board sponsored an open debate on the subject that spring. I saw flyers and posters all over campus. Everyone who came to the program was going to be asked to choose a side—pro or con— when they came in. Seating would be set up on opposite sides of the room. Everyone would listen to the arguments and, at the end, audience members would be given a chance to switch sides if their minds had been changed. Whichever side swayed the most opinions would win.

I couldn't see any way *I* could win. So I stayed home the night of that public debate.

One reason the death penalty controversy wouldn't die was because the executions continued. The Harveys called again to ask if I wanted to join them outside the gates of Angola to celebrate the next one.

Obviously, they had found no closure, no sense of peace in Robert Willie's death. Every bit of the grief and pain they'd felt for years was still eating at them. That made me sad. But in a strange sort of way it also made me feel grateful. I realized that seeing the effects of their abiding anger and hatred had helped convince me I needed to let go of those feelings myself. As weird as this may seem, I doubted I would have ever tried to forgive Robert Willie if it hadn't been for my unsettling exposure to such an all-consuming bitterness. I wished I could share with the Harveys the lesson I had learned. I would have tried to tell them that what little closure I had managed to find seemed directly related to that willingness to forgive Robert Willie. But they weren't ready or willing to hear that.

Unfortunately, the Harveys weren't the only people who were keeping the past very much alive in my mind. Some did it inadvertently.

I remember one evening that spring when Chris and I had dinner at the Blossman condo with two of his brothers and their girlfriends. The Blossman boys were so close that Gary and Donna, along with Reb and Michelle, were some of our best friends; we did a lot of things together. Reb, which stood for Roy Edward Blossman, a brilliant student near the top of his law school class, told us about a case he'd read that day. "I can't believe I didn't know anything about it. It happened back in 1980. These two guys kidnapped a young couple right off the Madisonville waterfront."

I looked up and caught the eye of Chris's brother Gary, who was sitting directly across the table from me. He had just taken a bite and his face immediately froze in a cross between a half-smile and a look of shock. I knew he knew, but he didn't know how to stop his brother. I sensed rather than saw Chris's reaction beside me. It took Donna and Michelle a split second longer to realize what Reb was talking about, but they too knew what had happened to me.

"It really was quite a story," Reb blundered on. "Did y'all know about it?"

Gary never broke eye contact with me as he said, "Yeah, we heard about it."

"Where was I?" Reb wondered. "I must have had my head buried in the books. But I still can't believe I didn't know about something that big happening right in our own backyard! These two guys . . ." and he began to retell the story. None of the rest of us knew what to say. We didn't want to embarrass him.

So the split second Reb paused in his narration, Gary changed the subject and we all began discussing something else entirely. The interruption may have seemed a little strange to Reb at the time, but when everyone else went right along, so did he. It wasn't until later that evening, after Chris and I headed back to campus, that Gary told Reb, "Debbie was that girl who got kidnapped."

He was so horribly embarrassed that when I saw him the next time a couple days later he apologized profusely. "Since I was the only one in the room who didn't know, I just wish someone would have stopped me!"

We ended up laughing together at the whole awkward situation. And it felt good that I could laugh.

This certainly wasn't the first time the case had been brought up in my presence by someone who had no clue about my involvement. A couple of times I'd had my feelings hurt because I'd elected to keep quiet and just listen to people who didn't know the facts come to judgmental conclusions about my case. "You know that never would have happened if they hadn't been parking out on that deserted lovers' lane!" or "They shouldn't have been out so late anyway." To the first statement I wanted to say, "That wasn't the way it was at all!" While I had to agree with the second statement, I always wanted to add, "So you think they deserved what happened to them because they were out later then they should have been? Isn't that a pretty high price to pay for missing curfew?"

After being offended and feeling I had to jump in and heatedly defend myself like that a couple times, I'd adopted a more proactive strategy. If people unknowingly began to discuss the case in my presence, I'd immediately speak up and acknowledge my involvement before they could stick their foot in their mouth.

Yet no matter which strategy I'd taken, people always seemed to feel bad. So this time, when I could honestly laugh off the awkwardness with Chris' brother, I felt I was making encouraging progress.

At the same time, it was one more experience that made me wonder whether I'd ever find complete closure and be able to outlive the consequences of my traumatic past.

Some of the irrational fears I'd struggled with for so long actually subsided a little after Robert Willie's death. My reactions became less fearful and more cautiously constructive. For example, I was still very leery of parking my car late at night in the unlighted lot behind the Kappa house and then hiking around to the front entrance alone in the dark. I accumulated more than my share of parking tickets when I parked on Lakeshore Drive in front of the sorority overnight and then didn't have time to move my car from that restricted area before rushing to make my 7:30 class the next morning. But I encouraged the other girls in the house to band together and look out for each other. "We should be careful," I'd tell them. "If one of us is going to be getting in late, we need to call or come to the front door to recruit a friend to ride with us or at least keep watch as we make the dark trek in from the parking lot."

Most of the girls would say, "You're right! We should do a better job of watching out for one other." Many of my sorority sisters listened because they understood and appreciated the reason for my caution.

I can honestly say I enjoyed the remainder of my time at LSU. I was especially loving the labs and the hands-on opportunities through which I was finally getting to work directly with kids in their classrooms.

The only real downside to the whole college experience was my ongoing struggle to pay for it. I worked at least one job every semester, and when money ran out I sometimes took a reduced load and worked a couple jobs. Two times I dropped out of school to work and save up for a semester. In the fall of '86 I took a reduced load so I could commute back and forth from home to help care for Poppie, whose health was failing rapidly. When he died early in 1987 I felt as if someone had ripped the cornerstone out of my life's emotional foundation. How much that loss had to do with what happened later that year, I'm not absolutely sure.

Chris studied in Innsbruck that summer and spent several weeks traveling around Europe. Part of me resented the fact that I couldn't afford such a trip and had to stay home working two jobs. During the day I was a teacher's aid helping in the classroom portion of the Job Training Partnership Act—a federally funded summer program for disadvantaged teenagers. At night I worked as a waitress in a Covington Restaurant called the Winner's Circle.

With Chris out of the picture for a few months I decided to explore a whole new social scene. A number of Winner's Circle employees would head over to New Orleans after the restaurant closed in the evening to take in the big city's bands and night life. I went with them. Most of them enjoyed drinking, and I found myself drinking with them.

Since my Texas adventure, I'd limited my drinking to an occasional beer or maybe a glass of wine when

Chris and I went out to eat at a nice restaurant. But I found it easy to slip back into old habits.

At least in part as a payback for Chris's leaving me for the summer, I dated a few other guys while he was gone—mostly older professional guys I met on the club scene. After years of steady dating with Chris, I got a real kick out of the change of pace.

Drinking wasn't ever a big part of Chris's life. Clubbing never appealed to him, nor was he a huge fan of New Orleans jazz. But I enjoyed all three. And I quickly learned I could have a very good time without him.

When Chris returned home that fall semester, he was ready to take up where we'd left off. I wasn't.

For months I'd felt a sense of growing restlessness about our relationship. Never enough to ever seriously consider leaving Chris, but enough that I'd begun to wonder if there wasn't something more I was missing. My summer of independence had only underscored those feelings.

I tried to talk Chris into going to New Orleans with me and my new friends. He went a time or two, but he didn't enjoy it. When I continued to go without him, he complained about me preferring my new friends' company to his. We also argued about my drinking.

Before long, our relationship was going from bad to worse. I don't know that either of us ever understood exactly why at the time. All I knew was that, after five years with Chris as a central part of my life, I had begun to wonder if I could make it on my own. So I took real satisfaction in exerting my newfound independence.

My mother's marital experience made independence seem doubly important. Time after time, I'd seen her look for self-fulfillment and find her sense of identity in some man, only to learn she couldn't rely on him to be there for the long run. I didn't want to make the same mistakes she had made. I needed to prove I could be my own person. I needed to be able and ready to take care of myself if, or rather when, Chris wasn't there.

To make matters worse, I think the insecure part of me that never quite believed that Chris truly loved me unconditionally wanted to test the limits of his love. That same part of me probably wanted to know if there was anyone else out there who *could* love me. Had I just settled for Chris because he'd been there at a time of my life when I'd been so emotionally vulnerable, so dependent? Did I even love Chris, or was it that I so desperately wanted the kind of security the Blossmans represented with their affluence and their happy, healthy, close-knit family?

Still, knowing how much he'd meant in my life for so long and always assuming a future together, why would I have these sudden questions and doubts? Chris didn't understand, and I certainly couldn't explain it to him.

When he tried to back off and give me a little emotional space, I wondered if that was an indication that he didn't really care, that he was finally pulling away. But when I thought he was holding on too tight, resisting my attempts at establishing independence, I'd resent what felt like control and determine to "show him"!

The poor guy couldn't win.

We argued a lot. But we never seemed to know why.

I felt like a boat tied to a solid, weatherbeaten dock. Chris was still there for me and had been for a long time. The old, knotted rope of our relationship bound me to him. But the ebb and flow of my own changing emotional tides would first pull me away and then bump me back. One minute the rope represented security and safe mooring, the next it felt like the only thing preventing me from sailing away to discover a broader world.

Up and down. Push and pull. Back and forth. The more I stretched and strained at the rope of our relationship, the farther Chris and I seemed to drift apart.

I guess he got fed up before I did.

Before I realized the mistake I'd made, it was June.

I think what really devastated me most was realizing how fast I had been replaced. For five years Chris and I had a relationship that had offered me the greatest sense of security and love I'd ever felt in my life. And just that fast it was gone. Chris had found someone else.

I felt hurt. *How could he do this to me? I thought I meant more to him!*

I felt stupid. *Look what I've done! And for what?*

I felt despair. *All that love and security. Gone. The only guy in the world who could ever love me like that. Gone. Five whole years of my life. Wasted.*

I still had one semester of school to go. So what did I do? I went home to work for the summer, determined once more to get on with life. This time without Chris.

For the second year in a row I worked as a teacher's aid with JTPA during the day and waited tables at night. It was only natural to slip back into the New Orleans night club scene with my friends. The drinking dulled the pain.

I lived with my mom and her new husband, John, that summer, in the spare bedroom of their condominium in Slidell. One August morning when my alarm went off and I didn't get up, Mom came into my room to check on me. She knew I'd gone out the night before; she also knew a hangover when she saw one.

"Debbie," she said. "Turn off your alarm. It's time to get up."

"Just leave me alone," I mumbled.

"You've got work this morning."

I opened my eyes only long enough to see numbers on the clock. But the red glare of their glow seemed more than my pounding head could absorb. I groaned, "Call and tell 'em I'm sick."

Mom, who'd been on the wagon herself for several years now, refused to do that. "You'll have to call them yourself," she told me. Then she walked out of the room and closed the door behind her.

The next time I opened my eyes it was almost noon, and I was trying to remember what had happened. I'd gone to a local night club with friends; I remembered that. We'd been having a good time; I remembered that. Of course, I also remembered we'd been drinking. But what happened later, where we went, who I was with, when or how I got home—I had absolutely no idea.

It was only the second time in my life I'd experienced a blackout. But the moment I realized it, I felt the same horrible, sick sensation I had when it happened the first time back in Texas—when I was eighteen and had just dropped out of high school. Only this time it was worse.

This time I couldn't say it never happened before. This time I saw the pattern: once again I was using alcohol to help me cope with emotional turmoil in my life. This time I realized I was doing what I'd seen my mother do—the very thing I'd sworn all my life I'd never do. This time I realized six years had passed since the last time and I still couldn't cope with my unhappiness and my depression; six years and nothing had changed.

Ever since my kidnapping, I'd felt that for some reason, for some purpose I hoped would become apparent one day, when Robert Willie and Joseph Vaccaro let me out of the car that Sunday morning by the Madisonville cemetery, I'd been given a second chance at life. Deep down in my heart I'd always believed God had given me that. And now I was about to blow that chance! I was throwing away that life.

I felt a terrifying sense of absolute despair. Total panic.

This time I couldn't blame Robert Willie. This time I knew the problem was me.

When I finally managed to climb out of bed, I went looking for my mother and found her in the kitchen.

"I had a blackout last night," I told her.

She said she could tell.

"I need help!"

She knew that too.

"Professional help."

She nodded. "I think you probably do."

Mom actually worked as the business manager of a local substance abuse treatment center. We agreed, for a variety of reasons, that I ought to go a little farther from home.

The very next day I checked myself into a thirty-day treatment program at a Baton Rouge hospital Mom recommended. The no-nonsense counselors there very quickly confirmed what I already knew and readily admitted: I had a drinking problem.

They also told me something I had to admit: I was full of suppressed anger and resentment.

And that eventually forced me to admit something I'd tried for years not to think about: an awful lot of my anger and resentment was directed at God.

As a kid and as a young teenager I believed in him. I trusted him. And then he let me down. Okay, maybe he saved me and gave me another chance at life. But what about all the pain and unhappiness I've gone through? Look at the mess I've made of things. Where was the Almighty in all that? If he really, truly loved me like the Bible claims, why would he let me go through all the heartache and suffering I've been through? Of course I'm angry! Why shouldn't I be angry at God? Why ...

At some point this troubling truth hit me: I'd found it easier to forgive Robert Willie than it was to forgive God.

Maybe it was because I thought God should be held to a higher standard. Or maybe I was still in too much pain from the past. Too frustrated by my present depression. Too afraid of facing the future.

Whatever the reason, I wasn't ready or able to let go of my anger with God. I wasn't sure I ever would be.

CHAPTER FOURTEEN

Undeserved Love

God wasn't the only one I still hadn't forgiven.

Eventually, I opened up enough to admit to the counselors I was angry with my mother about lots of things: our family's instability; our chronic financial straits; her history of irresponsible behavior and what I judged as her failure to accept parental responsibility. Much of my anger focused on the fact that she hadn't been home the night of the kidnapping—just as she hadn't been there for me so many other times when I felt I'd needed a mother.

"You should tell your mom how you feel," the counselors said.

"I can't do that," I told them. *It's hard enough admitting it to myself. Mom doesn't want to hear that.*

"She may not want to hear it. But she needs to hear it."

I wasn't so sure. *What good will it do?*

"Even if she's not ready to hear what you have to say, it will help you to say it."

I wasn't convinced, but they gave me no choice. Family therapy sessions were part of my treatment. They began three weeks into the program.

Still, it wasn't easy. In fact, it felt a little artificial, and more than a little strained, to confront such long-standing, personal issues in a conference room full of people—most of whom were complete strangers. Family therapy sessions not only included the other five or six patients who comprised my therapy group, but their family members as well. For someone like me, a pro at pretending and bottling up my deepest feelings, talking about such things in public seemed terribly awkward and painful.

The therapist primed everyone ahead of time—explaining the importance of "I" messages rather than "you" accusations, and of setting a goal of establishing open and honest communication patterns. So we all had a pretty good idea of the agenda.

At my counselor's urging, I admitted to my mom the anger I'd felt toward her. While I didn't go into great detail in front of those other people, I did tell her, through angry tears, how for so long I'd blamed her for what happened with the kidnapping. That if she'd been a more responsible mother, waiting anxiously at home for me to get back from my date, Mark and I would never have even been on the riverfront that evening to be abducted.

Mom admitted she'd felt guilty about that very thing.

The counselor asked what I thought Mom needed to do to help restore our relationship. I said, "She's already taken some important first steps. She's quit drinking."

When the counselor asked my mother what she thought she needed from me, Mom choked out the words, "I need Debbie to forgive me."

He turned to me. "Will you do that?"

"I want to," I said, looking at Mom. "I'm willing to try."

We both had tears in our eyes by that point, but we each remained somewhat restrained. There was no big emotional scene, no embracing and weeping on each others' shoulder.

I think we'd both been through enough to want this to be a new beginning. We hoped it was. But even if it was, it was only a start. As I walked out of that hospital at the end of my thirty days, I knew we still had a long way to go.

I felt better than I had coming in, mostly because I felt so much more rested. Early on, I'd realized how exhausted I was. Months and years of pretending and covering up my feelings had worn me down to nothing. Just one month of honesty, of not having to hold up a facade, had rejuvenated me enough to begin believing that maybe, someday, I'd feel strong enough to address all the issues brought to light during the treatment program's therapy sessions.

For some time after that I became a regular attendee of Alcoholics Anonymous. But I noticed the people at AA who seemed to have their lives together were invariably those members who'd worked their way through the twelve-step recovery process at their own speed, not those who'd been forced through the steps on a pace dictated by the predetermined length of a particular treatment program or by the time limitations of their insurance coverage. It confirmed my thinking that, while the thirty-day treatment program I'd been through may have helped point the way and set the course for my recovery, I certainly wasn't there yet. It would take a lot more time to work through all my personal issues.

This seemed especially true whenever I heard people stand up in meetings and talk about the need to rely on a "Higher Power." Some of them seemed pretty fuzzy as to who or what "Higher Power" they should depend on. I wanted to jump up and say, "It's God! He's the higher power you need to turn to!" But then I'd be reminded that I wasn't exactly to the point of depending on him again myself. Where I'd once sensed the excitement of God's spirit at work in my life, I now felt only an aching emptiness. The presence of God was gone.

I felt guilty about that, but I kept telling myself, *That's more than I can deal with right now. First I've got to get my life back in order and finish college. Then maybe I can solve the problems between me and God.*

I worked that fall at "The Wish List," an exclusive shop my aunt owned over in Mandeville that sold expensive jewelry, upscale accessories, and other fine things. I put in many long hours at the shop because I loved the job. It also gave me something to do to take my mind off what I now believe was an ongoing battle with chronic depression.

I was working late one day when Chris Blossman's fiancée happened to stop in looking for Christmas gifts and decided to buy a designer rug that "would look perfect in our apartment." Though we'd only met a time or two, we immediately recognized each other. What might have been awkward seemed cordial enough. I think I even managed to ask how the wedding plans were going.

Seeing Chris's fiancée made me think of him and of all that I'd lost. Yet I didn't blame her for the way things turned out. I couldn't even blame him. It was all my fault, and I accepted that. In fact, I was already so resigned to the fact that the wedding itself came and went with little or no impact on my own emotional funk. I wasn't invited. Even so, I wished Chris and his new bride well.

Unfortunately, thinking about their good fortune and joy only underscored my unhappiness. I was twenty-four years old and my life was nothing like I'd imagined it would be at this point. Most of the friends I'd grown up with were married and establishing families and/or successful careers. I'd accomplished nothing so far. I hadn't even completed college. And when I did, I'd be starting all over again.

No wonder I was depressed. Looking back, I saw only a fearful pattern of failure. Things had seemed so bad for so long that I wondered if they could ever be good again.

My only remaining requirement for graduation from college was one semester of student teaching. I signed up to do that in the spring semester of 1989. I'd been sick with the flu the day everyone turned in their placement requests, so I got the student teaching assignment no one else wanted—at the toughest junior high school in the worst gang-ridden section of Baton Rouge.

Believe it or not, I loved the experience. I saw plenty of heartache. I visited one of my students in the hospital after he was shot in the stomach during a gang fight. It wasn't easy to balance firm discipline with compassion, toughness with caring, but I learned it's possible to earn respect when you do. I got so much satisfaction from my interaction with the kids in my classes that I volunteered to work in an after-school program teaching computer skills to at-risk girls.

When I started my student teaching experience, I viewed it as a chance to serve and know that I'd made a contribution to society. By the time I finished, I'd begun to see how a career of service would not have to be a one-way street. The fulfillment I felt, the lessons I learned, the self-confidence I gained seemed to dwarf any contributions I'd made to the lives of my students.

The experience did far more for me than I'd done for them. I knew then, these were the kinds of kids I wanted to work with the rest of my life.

The summer I graduated I received several job offers for the upcoming school year—not only from districts around the state, but throughout the southeast. Special-ed teachers were in great demand.

I seriously considered one job offer in South Florida. The thought of getting away from home and starting the next stage of my life a long day's drive removed from the memories of Madisonville seemed very appealing. But I was so broke I couldn't afford to move; I didn't have enough savings to live on until I got my first paycheck.

My only option was to go home and move back in with my mom and her husband until I could afford my own apartment. So that's what I did. And when I applied for a job with the St. Tammany Parish schools, I was offered a position that same afternoon—as the special-education teacher of a self-contained behavioral-disorder classroom for fourth through sixth graders at C. J. Schoen Middle School, where I'd gone to school myself in the fifth and sixth grades.

The principal, Lawton McKee, my new boss, had actually been my principal back then. The day I was hired he interviewed me in his office. He smiled as he told me, "I seem to remember the last time you sat in this office. Something about shooting a teacher with a squirt gun."

I grimaced. "I'd hoped you wouldn't remember that."

He laughed. "It was you and Kay Bratton and a bunch of boys, wasn't it?"

"You're right," I admitted. Mary Pratt Lobdell, who taught at C. J. Schoen back in my student days, had actually taken a bunch of us to the Ben Franklin Five-and-Dime after school one day to buy water pistols. What she intended to be a fun, after-hours activity turned into something else entirely when we all decided to smuggle our weapons into school the next day.

I was exchanging potshots in the hallway with one of my fellow conspirators when the oldest, meanest, most humorless teacher in the entire school just happened to step out of her classroom right into the line of fire. My last shot caught her flush on the back of the head. We were all busted.

Fifteen years later, Mr. McKee still remembered that incident. But he hired me anyway.

I encountered other old memories everywhere I turned in that school. One day during the first week or so of classes, as I was escorting my students into the cafeteria for lunch, I spotted a familiar figure eating lunch and talking with Mr. McKee. It was Terry Bankston, my old high school principal, who had become the superintendent of schools for the parish.

About the time I noticed him, Mr. Bankston looked up, recognized me, and came rushing over to give me a big, friendly hug. "Welcome back," he told me. "I'm glad you're teaching for us, Debbie. I'm especially glad to have you here at this school. How are you getting along?"

"So far, so good!" I told him. "In fact, I'm lovin' it."

He smiled and nodded. Then he looked me right in the eye and said, "You know, Debbie, I always knew you were going to make it. I can't tell you how happy I am you're here!"

I'd heard lots of horror stories about first-year teachers who really struggled, and I was prepared for a rough start. But teaching wasn't that way for me at all. I loved my job and my kids from the get-go.

I very quickly proved to myself, and to everyone else at the school, that I could do my job and do it well. It helped that my colleagues gave me positive feedback almost immediately. "I don't know what you're doing with those kids, Debbie, but keep it up. They're all doing so much better this year!" Even the kids, and most of their parents, responded well to me. For the first time in forever I felt a sense of purpose in my life, a growing self-confidence, and a rekindled sense of hope about the future.

When I got paid at month's end, I found a great little apartment in a neighborhood not many blocks from the school. It was even close enough that some of my students could ride their bikes over to visit me at home.

I grew especially attached to one ten-year-old boy named Michael. His mother worked on the weekends, leaving him to babysit and provide for his eight- and four-year-old brothers. Every Saturday morning he'd ride his bike to my place with his little brothers perched on the handlebars. I'd fix pancakes and we'd all eat breakfast together, sitting on the front steps of my apartment.

Michael was the most difficult student I had that year. Like many of the kids in my behavior disorder class, he had very little self-restraint and an almost complete lack of conscience. It was Michael and other kids like him who started me comparing my BD students to Robert Willie. Unless something happened to turn them around, I believed a lot of these kids were headed for the same sort of serious trouble a few years down the road. That realization not only gave me purpose, it instilled a sense of urgency into my work. I desperately wanted to make a difference. And some days I actually thought I saw a little progress.

For a time that fall, I felt the only drawback to my job was the location of the school itself—just across the street from my old church. Every day as I drove to work, every recess I went out to the playground, every time I looked out the windows on the north side of the school building, I saw that church. It reminded once again that things were not right between God and me.

The church building was a visible, daily reminder of my meaningful spiritual past and my almost nonexistent spiritual present. It brought to mind the relationships I'd developed in my youth group and with God—relationships which had meant so much to me at such a crucial point in my personal, social, and emotional development.

I'd admitted as much to myself the previous year when I'd gone through treatment and went for a while to AA meetings. Now that I'd gone a whole year without a drop of alcohol, and was feeling so much better about myself, I realized there was still a spiritual void in my life. No matter how hard I tried to ignore it, just seeing that church every day drove the truth home. It convicted me. I knew I hadn't read the Bible or prayed regularly for years. I knew I wasn't living in God's will. And I realized deep down in my heart a part of me still believed, or at least *wanted* to believe, that God loved me and had a wonderful plan for me. If that was true, I had a lot to feel guilty about for wasting so many years of my life, for having neglected the relationships I once had.

So what's keeping me from returning to church? It was right there across the street—every day. *From turning back toward God?* I knew he was even closer than that.

Eventually, the old memories of what I once knew, plus the inner longing for something I still needed, prevailed over the guilt, the anger, and the questions that had kept me away for so long. One Sunday morning that fall I got up and decided to go to church.

I saw a lot of adults I recognized, but most of my old friends had moved on. There was, of course, a new group of young people. The church had grown and changed. And yet I sensed something familiar there.

I went back the next week. I think that was the Sunday I bumped into my principal, Mr. McKee, who acted pleasantly surprised to see me. "Why, Debbie, it's great to have you here today." Then he added, "You know, I'm the teacher of the College and Career Sunday school class. We'd love to have you join us next week."

I politely thanked him for the invitation without making any commitment. At the same time I was thinking, *Oh no! My boss just invited me to his Sunday school class. I'm not sure I'm ready to get that involved. How am I going to get out of this?*

I couldn't. I went to Sunday school and church the next week. And the week after. And the week after that. Before long, I was also involved in the church's singles group, which did include a couple people who'd been part of the youth group with me when I was a teenager. As I began to do things with them, as I gradually got more and more involved in the regular activities of the church, I felt that old familiar sense of "belonging" again. I had to admit I should have listened to my mom. Time and again for years, whenever she'd sense I was really struggling and discouraged, she would say to me, "Maybe you need to go back to church, Debbie. You always seemed happier back when you were involved in that youth group." Spiritual advice from a woman who didn't go to church herself may have been part of the reason I hadn't listened. *Come to find out, she was right all along!*

At church one day, reminiscing with a couple former members of the youth group, we were laughing over some story involving our old friends Bo and Brad Morris when I asked what anyone knew about them. Someone said Bo was married but Brad was still single, living up north somewhere and flying planes for some big airline. Those two guys had always been such a vital, central part of everything that went on in our youth group, that the more I remembered those old days, the more I wondered how they were doing, and the more I wanted to retrace and perhaps restore some of my spiritual roots by reminiscing with them.

Their parents, Ed and Judy Morris, remained pillars in the church. The next week I introduced myself (they remembered who I was) and asked about their boys. I learned Bo was indeed married and that Brad was now a pilot living in Pennsylvania. I told the Morrises how a few of us from the old youth group had been talking recently and I'd thought it would be nice to get back in touch. I asked for Brad's phone number so I could maybe call and chat about old times. His mom apologized, saying she didn't have the number with her that day. I'd have to get it another time.

When I asked again a few weeks later, she said she'd try to remember to bring it along to church with her the following week. But she didn't. And by the time I'd asked three or four times I started thinking maybe Judy Morris, for some reason, didn't want me calling her son.

It was winter already when a bunch of us were recounting old stories again. Reminded once more of Brad Morris, I picked up the phone and called his mom at home where she had no excuse not to give his number.

I called Brad immediately. Naturally, he was surprised to hear from me. We'd only seen each other once in the past eight, maybe nine years, when I'd bumped into him in a grocery store one summer during college. We'd said "Hi." Brad had asked, "Are you still goin' with that Blossman boy?" I'd told him I was. We'd chatted another sixty seconds or so, then told each other "See ya!" and went our separate ways.

This time, on the phone, we talked for more than an hour. I told him where I was teaching now. He told me a little about his job as an airline captain, flying commuter planes for USAir. But mostly we just laughed and talked and remembered the fun times we'd shared in our church youth group back in junior and senior high school.

Before we ended our conversation Brad asked, "You still datin' that Blossman boy?" I told him no, that Chris was actually married now. And then we hung up, with mutual promises to stay in touch and maybe try to get together with some of our old friends next time Brad made it home.

We talked a couple more times on the phone over the next few weeks, and when I went to Colorado over spring break as a chaperone for the church youth group's annual ski trip, Brad surprised me by showing up out there.

In some ways he was the same old Brad, with the same open, fun-loving, straight-ahead personality that always seemed so befitting his burly linebacker's physique. Growing up, Brad had always seemed to me, for lack of a better way to explain it, to be "all boy." More action than thought. Up-front and unsophisticated. More concerned with living life than sitting around contemplating its meaning. For all these reasons, he was a guy who, as popular as he was in high school, never quite mastered a smooth or comfortable routine with the girls.

Little of that seemed to have changed over the years. He still had the same physical presence and confident bearing of an athlete. He still laughed easily. He still seemed open and honest. There were still no airs, no pretensions about him. Even as an airline pilot, he'd acquired none of the smooth, practiced approaches usually perfected by guys who thought they defined "ladies' man." With Brad, it seemed, what you saw was what you got.

Yet I sensed a subtle change in him I couldn't quite put my finger on. By the end of our week together in Colorado I could only attribute the change to maturity. Brad's. Maybe even some of my own.

It was evident to me that this old friend, this person who'd been "all boy" was now "all man." It was just as obvious that this guy I'd always known had a crush on me when we were thirteen was falling for me again now.

I wasn't sure how I felt about that, but I was willing to find out. I invited Brad to Louisiana for a big music festival in New Orleans the next month. He flew home almost every weekend after that and by summer I knew, without a doubt, I was falling for him as well.

At this point, I was also a very different person from the Debbie Cuevas of my past. Very different even from the excited but uncertain rookie teacher who'd walked into her C. J. Schoen Middle School classroom for the first time less than a year ago. The personal growth and confidence I'd achieved through my professional success, bolstered by the gradual and ongoing rediscovery and restoration of my spiritual roots, had transformed my feelings about myself and my life. So I too had changed—just in time for Brad to meet and fall in love with the "new, improved me."

When I thought about it, I doubted Brad could have fallen for the "old me." Yet I realized the "old Debbie" was still very much a part of who I was. I thought that if Brad was as serious about me as he seemed, he deserved to know all about my past. And if I was getting as serious as I felt about him, I needed to know that he could accept that "old me," that he could love me unconditionally for *who I had been* as well as *who I was now.*

I decided I shouldn't wait any longer to find out. I not only owed it to Brad, I didn't want to risk being hurt anymore if honesty resulted in the end of our suddenly-blossoming relationship.

The next weekend Brad flew home, I invited him over for Saturday night supper at the house where I was then living with Mom and my sister, Dionne. Earlier that spring, when Mom had separated from her fourth husband, John, she had needed a place to live. The three of us decided we could economize, and maybe even benefit financially, if we'd all kick in and rent a house together. So I'd given up my apartment and moved into the small house we found in another section of Covington.

Not long after we finished supper, Mom and Dionne headed off to their rooms, leaving Brad and me alone in the living room. I knew what I needed to do, but I had no idea what I was going to say. Until I took a deep breath and told Brad, "Before you and I go any farther, before this relationship gets any more serious, there are some things you probably need to know about me."

He already knew the basic details of the kidnapping and the rapes. He'd been the only person I'd actually let read my initial deposition at the time. But he knew little or nothing that had happened over the intervening years. So I told him. Everything.

I recounted how I'd felt through the trials and afterwards. I told him about all the fears and failures. I talked about my five-year relationship with Chris, what all that had meant to me, and how I'd allowed my own insecurities and problems to destroy what Chris and I thought we had together. I confessed about the drinking problems, the blackouts, the panic that had prompted me to check into a substance abuse treatment center, and about going to AA for a while. I admitted the anger I'd felt for so long, not just toward Robert Willie, but toward my mom, and toward God. I even told Brad about the struggle I'd been having with depression in recent months.

The longer I talked, the heavier the load it felt like I was dumping on him and the more obvious it was to him, and felt to me, that I'd made a real mess of my life.

By the time I finished, I told Brad, "I'm sorry to unload all this on you at once. But I wanted you to know. If it means you decide you don't want to get any more involved with someone who comes with so much heavy baggage, I'll be sorry but I'll understand. You don't have to say anything now; I know I've given you a lot to think about."

Brad remained quiet and thoughtful for a just a few seconds before he acknowledged, "There is a lot to think about. And I promise I will do that. But nothing that you've told me tonight changes the fact that I love you, so I don't think there's anything you've said that we can't deal with and work through."

As thrilled as I was to hear him say that, as much as I wanted to believe it, I knew he needed more time. "If you decide not to pick me up for church in the morning, I'll know why," I told him.

He assured me he would.

And he did.

After church we talked some more. In the bright light of day he reiterated what he'd said the night before. He didn't think I'd told him anything that would change his mind.

Brad had already done a lot of thinking in just a few short hours. He admitted some of what I'd said raised questions he thought we needed to address. Mostly his concerns centered around the possibility of recurring emotional problems. If the depression returned, if the irrational fears cropped up again, if I exhibited evidence of unresolved anger or displayed serious insecurities, what would we do? When would we know there was a problem we needed to address? How would we deal with it? What should he do to try to help me? Would I be willing to seek professional help again if I needed to? Who would decide when that might be necessary?

Like any good pilot, Brad had a safety checklist he wanted to run through. While I could have been discouraged at the number of questions, it was much more encouraging to know he was carefully considering the options. By the time we finished calmly discussing his concerns that afternoon, when he kissed me goodbye at the airport and promised, "See you next week," I knew he still believed we had a future together. And so did I.

Over the next few months I learned anew that there is no feeling in the world that provides a greater sense of security than believing you are accepted unconditionally by someone who knows all there is to know about you and loves you anyway. Brad loved me like that. And for that reason I knew, beyond a shadow of doubt, that God had brought him into my life as part of his grand design. After so many years wandering an emotional desert, I could finally see the Promised Land.

Brad officially proposed when we went skiing out in Colorado with his parents and our pastor and his wife, in February of 1991. We got married in August of that year and moved to Baltimore, where Brad had just been based.

I taught special education in yet another wonderful setting that afforded me recognition and appreciation while enabling me to really stretch and grow professionally at the same time. We bought a home and began building our marriage. And I decided that with the healing effects of passing time, and with the restorative power of God's grace as defined for me and delivered to me by way of my wonderful husband's unconditional, overwhelming, and undeserved love, I had finally managed to put my troubled past behind me forever.

I thought wrong.

CHAPTER FIFTEEN

That Nun Wrote a Book

L ife did go on.

Dionne called our Baltimore home one evening in 1993. "You may want to sit down, Deb," she told me. My little sister always did have a tendency to be overly dramatic.

"What is it, Dee?"

"Are you sitting down? I found out something today. And you're not gonna want to hear it."

"What is it?"

"That nun wrote a book."

"What . . . Who?"

"You know, whatshername, Sister Helen Prejean. She wrote a book."

I couldn't believe it. "About what?"

"All about her relationship with Robert Willie and another guy on death row. I saw it when I was in a bookstore today. I didn't want to pay for such junk, but I stood there in the aisle reading it so long the clerks started giving me funny looks. So I bought it and brought it home. I told Mom you'd probably never see it. But we figured if you ever did, it'd be better for you to hear about it from us first.

"The book's called *Dead Man Walking*. And while it tells some about Faith Hathaway's murder, it doesn't really focus much on what happened to you or on your legal case. I haven't even found your name in the book yet . . . I still haven't read it all. But so far, it just sounds to me like this Sister Prejean felt sorry for Robert Willie and wrote a book to try to get other people to feel sorry for him, too."

I thought, *At least my name isn't in the book.* But I couldn't believe there was a book written about Robert Willie. *What more is there to tell?*

"After you finish, send me the book," I told Dionne. "I want to see it." It angered me to think anyone had written a book about Robert Willie and hadn't seen fit to ever talk to me.

When the book arrived I showed it to Brad; he didn't want me to read it. "It's over," he reasoned. "Why open yourself to all that pain and emotion again?" He wanted me to throw it away and forget it.

He didn't say so, but I knew he worried about how I'd react and was wondering what he'd have to do if reading the book sent me off the deep end again emotionally. But I felt sure I could handle it. So I put the book away, with plans to read it when Brad was out of town.

Much of what Helen Prejean wrote had little to do with me or my case, yet some of what I read did make me angry. I was particularly bothered by the way she simply quoted Robert Willie, making himself sound like he'd been the follower and Joseph Vaccaro the instigator of all they did. She never offered any other, differing perspective—which she could have easily gotten by interviewing the investigators, talking to me, or simply referring to the trial transcripts. The fact that she just took Robert Willie's word made it feel to me as if the book was discounting everything I'd testified to during the trials. And that made me very angry.

As a school teacher, I was also irritated at the clear inferences made that the "system" had somehow failed Robert Willie. She implied that he'd ended up where he did, first because the schools let him slip through the cracks and then because the legal system I'd cooperated with abused his human rights by condemning him to execution. *What about his responsibility for his own actions?* I thought.

I didn't read the whole book. I stopped before I got to the part describing the execution itself. I reasoned, *I've already dealt with that and with my own part in that. I don't need to dig all that up again by looking at it from her perspective. I don't need or deserve any more pain.* While I was still a little curious to know whether or not Robert Willie expressed any remorse at the end, I didn't want to learn that he didn't. So I quit reading and actually left the book under the seat of my car.

I knew I hadn't seen any reviews or advertisements for the book, so it didn't figure to be a very big seller. I could probably forget about it and never have to think about it again.

However, one afternoon a few weeks later, I was out in the front yard when one of our neighbors from a couple doors down walked over to pass the time of day. "I've just been reading a book that took place down in your neck of the woods," Bernie said.

"Is that so?" I responded, knowing Louisiana made for a colorful setting in countless books.

"Yep. It's about this nun who works with prisoners on death row. The book's called *Dead Man Walking*. Ever hear about it?"

"As a matter of fact, I think maybe I have," I admitted. But I didn't tell him I'd read part of it. Or that the book was still under my car seat. Nor did I mention my personal connection to the story.

But I did think to myself, *I can't believe this. More than a dozen years have gone by. I'm living one thousand miles from Madisonville. And here my neighbor brings this up out of the blue. When is it ever going to end?*

More life went on. And I was able to pretty much forget the book *Dead Man Walking* in the excitement of expecting my first child.

Our son, Conner, was delivered in September of 1994. When Mom came to be with us for a week she and I made great strides forward in our relationship.

I know that the birth of her first baby is a milestone in every woman's relationship with her mother. There's a deeper understanding of love, a broader perspective on life, a new sense of sisterhood, and a shared bond of experience that simply didn't exist before. And I think Mom and I both felt that.

But something else happened there, too. For one whole wonderful, exciting, exhausting week, my mother doted on me and helped me take care of my newborn son. As an anxious first-time parent, it amazed me to watch the calm confidence of an experienced mom, my mother, at work. She instinctively knew exactly what to do with Conner and she managed to take total care of me at the same time. She was there for me in a way I'd never known, or at least never felt, in my entire life.

I remember thinking, *As angry as I've been with her in the past, she's being a great mom now. And she's obviously going to be a wonderful grandmother to my son.*

When the time came to hug her good-bye, I cried. I didn't want to let go.

Becoming a parent broadened my perspective on a lot of things.

I remember standing by the crib, looking down at my sweet, sleeping son, and suddenly thinking, *Robert Willie was a baby once. What happened? How does a helpless, innocent, impressionable infant become the kind of person who would inflict such heartless cruelty and evil on other human beings?*

Sometimes as I held my precious baby boy in my arms and gazed adoringly into his bright and curious eyes, I thought too of Robert Willie's mother, Elizabeth Oalmann. And I wondered what dreams she'd harbored in her heart for her firstborn son. *Did she hold him in her arms like this? Did she love her little boy like I loved mine?*

Those questions reminded me of an incident that had taken place the very first year I was teaching. I'd been complaining one afternoon to the school secretary about the failure of a mother of one of my students to show up for a scheduled parent-teacher conference. Irritated that I'd stayed after school only to be stood up, I said rather caustically, "I bet if I'd have promised free cigarettes she would have been here!"

When my principal, Lawton McKee, overheard what I said, he called me into his office and asked me to sit down. "You need to understand something, Debbie," he began rather sternly. "Not all the parents of your students are going to have the same values you and I do. They may not be raising their families the way we would. They may not qualify as 'good parents' by our standards. They may even be a big part of the reason their kids have the kind of problems your students have. But . . . ," he leaned forward and looked right in my eyes, "don't ever make the mistake of thinking these parents don't love their kids. Because they do!

"They may not show up for things like parent-teacher conferences and PTA meetings. But if they think their child is hurt or being treated unfairly, you'll see how much they care and how much they do love their children."

That had been an important lesson for such an idealistic and judgmental young teacher to learn. I took those words to heart and soon learned how right they were. When I opened my mind as well as my eyes I could see every parent's love. Yet I didn't really begin to understand the true nature of parental love until I had a child of my own.

For years I'd viewed Elizabeth Oalmann with a judgmental mixture of fear and hard feelings. Not only had she created and raised a monster capable of such atrocities, but even after the vicious crimes he committed, she'd helped him escape and perjured herself on the witness stand in a desperate attempt to get him off. *If she'd do that,* I thought, *what were the chances she would want revenge on the girl whose testimony condemned her son to death?*

It wasn't until Conner was born that I knew for myself the instinctive, almost desperate nature of a mother's love—a love so deep, so unshakable, it will see and do and believe almost anything for a child.

It was only then, after I had a son of my own, that I began to understand Mrs. Oalmann. Only then that I remembered and fully appreciated something else that happened during the trials.

Robert's mother had lied for him in court. She'd told everyone who would listen that he wasn't capable of doing the things he'd been accused of doing. She'd defended him at every turn. But when the tape of his confession was played in court, when she heard the horrible details recounted in her son's own words, she'd finally broken down, and had to leave the courtroom. Mark Brewster's Aunt Joyce, who'd been a secretary at Madisonville Junior High when Robert Willie was a student, just happened to be in the courthouse hallway to witness Mrs. Oalmann's tears. And when Robert Willie's mom looked up and recognized Joyce, she said, "Tell that little girl I'm so sorry."

I didn't accept that from Robert Willie's mother at the time. But I could now. As a mother myself, I finally understood how painfully heartbreaking that whole experience had to be for her. And I could finally forgive her.

One evening in the late spring or early summer of 1995 Dionne called again to say, "You better sit down, Debbie." She went on to tell me she'd been watching the local evening news on a New Orlean's station when she heard that there was a movie being made based on Helen Prejean's book.

"You're kidding! When's it coming out? Who's in it?"

"I don't know," Dionne told me. "I wasn't paying that much attention until I heard them mention *Dead Man Walking.*"

Maybe it'll turn out to be nothing, I told myself. *The book didn't make that big a splash.*

A few nights later Dionne called back. She'd been watching *Entertainment Tonight* and heard more about the movie: "Tim Robbins is directing it. And guess who's starring in it."

"Who?"

"Susan Sarandon and ... you're not gonna believe this ... Sean Penn."

"Sean Penn?" When I heard that I needed to sit down.

"Just like you always said, Debbie. Is that unbelievable or what?"

Yes, it's unbelievable. Years before, when Sean Penn had been the hot young actor making headlines by punching out paparazzi and marrying Madonna, I'd seen the advertisement for one of his movies. In the film he'd played a scruffy looking character who bore an uncanny resemblance to Robert Willie. It was such a disturbing, almost chilling likeness that I decided I didn't want to see the picture. Several times after that, whenever I saw him featured in a magazine or in some film clip on TV, I'd said to various family members, "If they ever made a movie of my story, they would have to get Sean Penn to play Robert Willie."

But I'd always been joking. I never for a moment thought anyone would make a movie, let alone a movie involving people like Tim Robbins, Susan Sarandon, and Sean Penn. With names like that, I knew this had the potential of becoming a major motion picture.

And then what?

I didn't know. That scared me. And my fear translated into anger that I was going to have to deal with all this yet one more time. That someone, anyone, had the power, or thought they had the right, to resurrect those old painful memories again—this time in the name of entertainment and profit.

As upset as I'd been to learn about the book, this was worse. The book had turned out to be little more than a blip on the radar screen of public awareness; it hadn't personally affected me much at all. But a major motion picture was bound to make headlines and create widespread curiosity about the story behind the movie. If that happened, I might get caught in the media glare and I didn't know how that might impact me or my family.

I worried so much about what little I'd heard that I decided to see if I could learn anything more that might set my mind at ease. I called information to get the name of Butch Badon and then called him at home. Butch was the newspaper reporter who had covered my story from the kidnapping through the trials, first for the *New Orleans Times-Picayune* and later for the local *St. Tammany News-Banner*.

I'd never in my life talked to Butch Badon. I wasn't even sure how to explain who I was or why I was calling until I heard a voice answer on the other end of the line. "Hello?"

"Butch Badon, please."

"Speaking."

"Mr. Badon, I don't know if you would remember me, but a long time ago when you wrote about me, you referred to me as a 'sixteen-year-old girl from Madisonville'. I'm . . ."

"Of course, I know who you are," he interrupted. "You're Debbie Cuevas! I can't believe I'm finally getting to talk with you!" Naturally he wondered why I was calling him after fifteen years.

I explained that I was married and lived up in Maryland now, but that I still had family in Madisonville and my sister had heard about the plans for the movie. I told him I was wondering how Hollywood was going to portray the story and was calling to find out if he could tell me any more about it.

"As a matter of fact, I can," he said. His paper had reported the story from the time the movie production people showed up to scout out locations. He confirmed that Susan Sarandon was playing Helen Prejean. But he told me Sean Penn was to play a composite character representing both men for whom the nun had served as spiritual advisor—Patrick Sonnier and Robert Willie. The details of their crimes had been combined and Penn's character had been given a different name. In fact, he told me, all the names used in the movie, except for Helen Prejean's, would be fictional names.

I was somewhat relieved to hear all this. Maybe the movie wouldn't become a major intrusion on my life after all.

When Butch Badon had answered all the questions I had for him, as I was thanking him and just about to say goodbye, he said: "As long as I've got you on the line, do you mind if I ask you a couple questions? There are some things about the case I've always wondered about."

"Okay," I replied. I figured I owed him that much.

We spent another half hour talking. He said he'd always wondered about the depositions where I'd talked about engaging the kidnappers in conversation. So I told him some of the things we'd talked about. He asked for my impressions of the two kidnappers. And he asked, "Why do you think they ever let you go?"

I told him a lot of people had concluded I was just lucky. But I didn't believe in luck. The FBI had told me there was no earthly reason they could understand that I'd been allowed to live. As far as I was concerned, the only thing I could say for certain was that it had been the grace of God—that he had kept me alive for a purpose.

What Robert Willie was thinking, why he would have let me go like he did, I could only speculate. I told Butch I thought things became complicated when Tommy Holden got involved and let Willie and Vaccaro know he wasn't going to be a party to kidnapping or murder. But I've always believed that by staying calm, I bought enough time to create some conflict in Robert Willie's mind. He actually did start to like me and when he started to think about me like that, it was a lot harder for him to do to me what he'd planned to do—which was what he'd done to Faith Hathaway.

When I'd answered all Butch's questions as best I could, I thanked him for the information and for his time. He told me he'd thought about me a lot of times over the years and he was just glad to finally have the chance to talk. He wished me well and we said our good-byes.

While I wondered in the weeks and months that followed what was happening with the plans for the movie, I didn't worry about its impact on me quite as much after that.

There were a lot of bigger things going on in our personal lives during that time. Like moving. And changing jobs.

Brad's dream had always been to fly big jets. But as a pilot with USAir's commuter line, that wasn't going to happen anytime soon. So in the summer of 1995, when he got a job offer from DHL, the worldwide delivery company, as flight engineer flying 727s, we agreed he should go for it. The downside was that in giving up his seniority, plus exchanging his captain's seat for that of a flight engineer, he had to take such a drastic cut in pay that we couldn't afford the mortgage payments on our home in Maryland. So we rented out our house and moved temporarily back to Louisiana, where we lived in a tiny condo while Brad commuted back and forth (like a lot of pilots) to DHL's headquarters in Cincinnati.

I took another teaching job that wasn't nearly as fulfilling personally or professionally as the one I gave up in Maryland. And Brad was gone from home more of the time. I felt lonely and missed all my Maryland friends. And we had to make do on a shoestring budget. Whenever Brad was home I complained about all these things. It was in many ways the unhappiest, most stressful time in our entire marriage.

The only really good thing about it was that we attended church again every week there in Covington— at the church where we'd grown up. For a lot of reasons we'd never found a church we felt comfortable in where we lived in Maryland. Quickly, we realized what we'd been missing.

Each Sunday we felt spiritually challenged and encouraged, either by pastor Waylon Bailey's sermons or by the lively discussion in our Sunday school Bible study. Or both. It seemed every week there was some little thing that spoke directly to us and the every-day struggles we were going through—whether it was the loneliness I was feeling, the uncertainty and unsettledness Brad and I felt about the future, the financial insecurity we faced, or whatever. I can't count the number of times that summer and fall when we got in our car after church, looked at each other and said, "Do you think anybody else is getting anything out of this? Or is God just speaking directly to us?" Week after week there was always something that made us feel, *Wow! We were obviously meant to be here today!*

One time there was a lesson on prayer. Another time I heard some very relevant truth about trusting God. Another time we talked about seeking and knowing God's will.

Some of what I heard I'd known and believed before—I just needed to be reminded. Others were new thoughts entirely. Taken individually they were each fairly small things, but they added up to some very big realizations—that God really did care enough about us to want to speak to us; that he was concerned about our smallest problems as well as our biggest needs; that if we were to put ourselves in a position to grow spiritually he would help us do that; and if all that was true, it meant—and this was the most important truth of all—we could trust God with both the doubts and the details of our lives.

As all this began to slowly sink in, I noticed a distinct shift in my attitude toward my Heavenly Father. For years virtually all my interactions with him had been focused on my angry "why?" questions. *Why me? Why did you let Robert Willie and Joseph Vaccaro do that to me? Why did you let my life get so messed up? Why didn't you intervene here or do that there? Why? Why? Why?*

Gradually, I realized I needed to change my accusatory tone and absolve God from the blame I'd been heaping on him: I needed to forgive God. Not because he'd done anything wrong. And not because *he* particularly needed *my* forgiveness. Not for his sake at all. But for my own sake. Because I needed to let go of the unforgiving spirit that had barred the door of my heart and kept his Spirit out.

As I did that, as my heart changed that fall, that Spirit gave me new insights. Looking back over everything that had happened to me, I realized God had never abandoned me the way I'd accused him of doing for so many years. He had been there all along—protecting me and providing for me.

I remembered the old black fisherman and his grandson who just happened to be walking along that desolate stretch of Fricke Road at the very time my kidnappers had taken me to the same deserted spot where they'd murdered and left Faith Hathaway only days earlier. When they'd disappeared without a trace I'd wondered, *Were they real? Or were they angels?* Real or not, I now realized God had used them like guardian angels to change Robert Willie's plan and keep me alive.

I remembered how terribly alone and forsaken by God I'd felt when I was finally taken to the pit of despair that was Tommy Holden's trailer. After everything I'd been through, being trapped in some two-bit drug dealer's squalid hideout had seemed the lowest of low points. And yet it had been Tommy Holden's "moral qualms" about killing me that triggered the dispute between my abductors that led to my release.

The more I thought about it, the more I looked back through my new faith-tinted lenses, the more I began to see. Not only had God been with me at my lowest, most desperate moments, he had uniquely equipped me to survive everything I'd been through. Before and since my horrible kidnapping ordeal.

For so many years I'd resented the family turmoil I'd endured as a child—the tension, the arguments, the anger that had conditioned me to tune out and withdraw into myself to escape unpleasantness and maintain for myself a measure of emotional control. Now I could see it was that same self-defense mechanism that enabled me not to panic but to keep enough of my wits about me to survive. God had used the experiences I'd most resented to help keep me alive.

He'd used people, too. Looking back I could see so many now. Family. Friends. Mark Brewster. Chris Blossman. Brad. Teachers. Administrators. My high school principal who promised to keep an eye on me and was superintendent of schools when I got my first job in a school that "just happened" to be across the street from my old church. *Yes. God was there working and watching all along.*

As I came to believe that, I found that the basic question I had for God changed as well. Instead of, "Why did this terrible thing happen?" I began asking, "What do you want me to do now in this situation?" Instead of complaining and asking God why he hadn't solved my problems, I began asking God what he wanted me to do and how he wanted to use the circumstances and experiences of my life.

I felt a growing sense of conviction that God did want to use me. And that there was something preventing that from happening. *But what?*

The answer to that question too came slowly over those months as Brad and I began to grow spiritually again. There was no lightning bolt from heaven. No sudden turning point. No single climactic moment to which I can look back and point. But over the course of weeks and months, I came to a very clear and very real understanding that I could never "get on with life," nor could I discover, or do, what God intended for my life because I had never been able to forgive the most central character in my personal drama. I'd forgiven Robert Willie and Joseph Vaccaro as best I could. I'd forgiven Robert Willie's mother. I'd forgiven my own mother. I'd even reached the point where I'd forgiven God. But I had not yet forgiven myself.

I realized that before I could do that, I had to feel that God had forgiven me. Which in turn meant I needed to ask his forgiveness.

Not that I still blamed myself for what happened with the kidnapping, but there was plenty I'd done wrong since. I'd made a mess of my life by doing so many things I should never have done, and not doing other things I knew I should do.

Until I asked God to forgive me for all those things, I could never feel forgiven. Nor could I forgive myself.

So that's what I did. Over a period of weeks, whenever I remembered something I'd done wrong, or something I hadn't done right, I simply prayed and asked God's forgiveness. When I remembered anything I'd done to hurt anyone, I asked God's forgiveness. When I realized I'd fouled up the priorities of my life, I told God I was sorry and asked him to help me set them straight. When I remembered an attitude I knew God didn't want me to have, I prayed for forgiveness.

As I did this, an incredible thing happened. As I came to know and feel God's forgiveness, it was suddenly easy to forgive myself. If God who is holy and perfect could forgive me, who was I to think I should hold myself to a higher standard? If he didn't blame me, neither could I!

What a new and incredible sense of freedom!

Still, I couldn't shake the growing sensation that there was something else I needed to do as well.

CHAPTER SIXTEEN

Confronting Sister Helen

We were in Texas visiting Brad's grandfather and staying in his uncle's home when the local media broke the story of a missing eight-year-old girl. The case made front-page headlines and led the evening newscasts on all the local television stations.

Since 1980, news reports of missing person or kidnapping cases had often triggered an emotional reaction in me. For some reason this little girl's story hit me especially hard. Over the two-day period of our visit, every time I heard an update on the radio or saw another TV report, I found myself imagining what might be happening and how terrified a kidnapped eight-year-old would be. I thought about her. I prayed for her. I just couldn't get her off my mind.

On the second day, we watched the evening news report to learn the little girl still hadn't been found. The news went to a commercial and suddenly, with no warning whatsoever, there on the screen, was a close-up shot of Sean Penn in a clip advertising the upcoming release of *Dead Man Walking*. It was like having Robert Willie right in that living room with me. After the emotional turmoil of the previous two days, I felt like someone had just kicked me in the stomach.

I was on the lookout for movie news after that. In December, the New Orleans press began talking about a local premier showing at the city's upscale Galleria Theaters during the Christmas holidays. The reports I saw said that Sister Helen Prejean would be there for the big opening-night ceremonies.

Even though I'd been dreading the attention I feared the movie would bring, I considered going on opening night. I tried to imagine what would happen if I just walked up to Sister Prejean and introduced myself. Not to make a scene; I never wanted to make a scene. But she'd always been so articulate, so sure of herself whenever I'd seen her interviewed on TV that I thought, *I'd like to see how she'd react if I caught her off-guard like I've been caught off-guard so many times over the years whenever she popped up in the news, on bookstores shelves, and now on the movie screen.*

I eventually decided against going. I even made a deliberate choice not to watch the news coverage on the night of the premier. But there was no way to avoid the reaction the movie begat over the next few days and weeks.

Everywhere I went, friends or acquaintances wanted to know what I thought about the movie. People were usually surprised when I told them I hadn't seen it and didn't know if I wanted to. Most of them assumed I knew the inside scoop. And people were always surprised to learn all that I knew about it I'd learned through the media, just as they had. "You mean they made a movie about your story and they didn't even talk to you or tell you what they were doing?"

That kind of reaction fueled my own resentment. I could tell myself, *The movie, like the book, isn't exactly my story,* but I kept wondering, *Didn't anybody ever think about my feelings, my reaction?*

One week in January another one of our Sunday school lessons spoke directly to me. It dealt with the question "What should we do when we feel we've been wronged? As Christians, how should we respond to people we feel have wronged us, intentionally or unintentionally?" I didn't contribute to the class discussion that day, but it certainly got me thinking.

I thought about the different people who had wronged me—who I'd tried to forgive. And I realized there were very different levels and degrees of hurt. The cruel, intentional way that Robert Willie and Joseph Vaccaro had hurt me was very different, for example, from the way I'd felt wronged by my mother. And the sense of forgiveness I felt was different as well.

But what about Helen Prejean? I didn't know her. I'd never so much as met her. I never once thought she intentionally did anything to hurt me. Yet I still felt a real sense of resentment toward her that troubled me. Many times over the years, in newspaper accounts and on television coverage, I noticed she often tried to balance her concern for the condemned by also calling for compassion for the victims. I'd read in her book how she'd tried in vain to reach out and try to comfort the Harveys.

And yet she hadn't ever contacted Mark or me. *Did that mean she didn't see us as victims, since we hadn't died?* There were lots of times when I thought dying would have been easier.

The fact that she'd never contacted me made me feel as if she'd simply dismissed me and everything that had happened to me. I realized that's what hurt, that's what I resented.

Maybe if I could talk to her. Woman to woman. Christian to Christian. If I could get a sense that she was genuine, that she had been truly trying to know and do God's will, just as I'm doing now, maybe then I could get over this feeling of resentment and forgive her, too.

I told Brad that. But neither of us could imagine how that might take place.

One night later that month, Brad was gone flying, and my sister, Dionne, came over to our condo to spend the evening with Conner and me. "When are you going to see the movie?" she wanted to know. "Are you planning to see it?"

"I'm not sure," I told her. "But I do kinda wish I could talk to Helen Prejean."

"Then why don't you call her?" Dionne asked.

"I can't just do that!"

"Why not?" my sister demanded.

"Well . . . for one thing I don't know her number . . ."

"Call information. Here, I'll do it . . ." Dionne walked over, picked up the phone, and began punching numbers. She spoke to the operator and quickly scribbled down a number. When she hung up, she brought me the phone and the piece of paper. "Now you can call her."

Before I had time for second thoughts, that's what I did. The phone rang. A woman's voice answered at the other end.

"Sister Prejean?" I asked.

"Yes."

"I'm Debbie Morris. You wouldn't recognize my name, but you might remember me as the 'sixteen-year-old girl from Madisonville'."

There was what seemed like an eternity of silence before she responded, "Debbie? Thank God you're alive!"

In that one phrase, I heard surprise and shock, uncertainty and disbelief. But I also heard something else. In the sound of her voice and the way she said my name, I felt Helen Prejean's compassion. I instantly sensed in her a genuine love for life and for people. For me.

"I hope I'm not calling at a bad time."

"Oh, no. This is fine," she quickly assured me.

I told her, "I've been wanting to talk to you for a very long time. I wondered if you would be willing to give me some time. Maybe we could get together and talk. I have some questions I'd like to ask you, and I have some things I'd like to share about my own experience that might interest and even surprise you."

She told me she'd very much like to do that. "I'm leaving town tomorrow for a week or so. My schedule has gone crazy since the release of the movie. But when I get back in New Orleans, I'll call you and set something up."

We chatted a few more minutes. I told her where I was living, that I was married and had a seventeen-month-old son. She told me a little about the speaking opportunities she'd had as a result of the movie.

Before we concluded our surprisingly cordial conversation, I decided I had to ask her one question. "Sister Helen," I began hesitantly, "I've always wondered why you never contacted me at all."

There was a long pause. "I should have reached out to you, Debbie. I'm sorry," she said. "I considered it, but your name was never mentioned in the press. You obviously chose to stay out of the limelight. I worried that you would feel my contacting you was a violation of your privacy. It certainly wasn't that I didn't care or hadn't considered what you went through.

"In fact," she continued, "I can't tell you the number of times over the years when I've thought about you, prayed for you, and hoped you were doing okay."

Even as she said those words, I believed her. I heard God's love in her voice. I knew she cared. I realized she *had* cared all along. My resentment melted away and I knew I could forgive her.

Sister Helen did call me when she got back in town. We agreed to meet at our condo. I baked carrot cake and fixed coffee.

Brad met her at the door and then retreated upstairs where Conner was napping, so just the two of us could talk. She didn't know much about my story, so I started at the beginning with the kidnapping itself.

I saw the pain on her face and in her eyes as she listened to me describe what had happened. I could tell she was empathizing and hurting for me. But I sensed she was also hurting for herself, because of her own relationship with Robert Willie. She had deliberately shielded herself from knowing many of the details at the time. *Maybe she couldn't have felt the same compassion or had the same kind of relationship with him if she had known—surely it would have been harder.* Clearly, hearing the story from my mouth, even now, was troubling for her.

She was intrigued when I told her about the conversation Robert Willie and I had about my dating requirements. She acted surprised that he'd shown that much vulnerability. She herself had seen only glimpses of it from time to time when he'd seemed like a desperate little boy behind his tough facade.

We laughed together at the absurdity of Robert Willie thinking I might still be his girlfriend. "You realize," Helen said, "he fancied himself quite a ladies' man."

"I know," I told her. "So much so that each time he raped me, when he finished, he wanted to know if I'd 'enjoyed' it."

"He actually asked you that?"

"He did."

She shook her head. "What did he expect you to say?" She paused, "What *did* you say?"

"I told him he was disgusting."

"Really? You said that?" She was amazed that I had stood up to Robert Willie like that. "He liked having people being scared of him." She seemed to think it was a pretty big deal that he had expressed any caring at all for me. "He just didn't do that sort of thing. It wasn't his nature."

I told her I'd always had questions about Robert Willie at the end. "Did he ever talk about me or about regretting what he'd done to me?"

Helen said she'd tried to bring up Mark's and my kidnapping a time or two in the context of trying to get Robert to assume some responsibility for the horrible things he'd done. "He told me, 'I know we should never have done that to those kids. They didn't deserve that.'"

"But did he show any real remorse before he died?" I asked. "Did you sense that he felt genuinely sorry? Or that he accepted responsibility for what he had done?"

She shook her head sadly. "No. And you know, Debbie, I'm not sure he was capable of that."

I went on to admit to Helen that she hadn't been the most popular person with my friends and family. That there had been many occasions over the years when I had wished she and her marches and her book and now her movie would have just gone away, so I'd never have to hear her name again. "But you know," I told her. "I'm glad now that didn't happen. I can see that your popping up from time to time forced me to confront some issues I needed to face. Without that, I might have buried some things that would have hurt me more in the long run. God has used you to give me opportunities to heal."

Knowing that Helen's book and now her movie had made her a world-renowned spokesperson against capital punishment, I admitted that I personally struggled with my own feelings about the death penalty. I told her that Robert Willie's death had definitely reduced the fear I had to live with, that while I wasn't at all sure that was justification enough to execute a man, I couldn't help the fact that I simply felt better knowing Robert Willie was dead.

Helen seemed to understand and accept that.

We talked about a lot of subjects that afternoon. We found other things that bound us besides our own unique connections with Robert Willie. We had each worked with disadvantaged kids and had both a love and a burden for doing that. We even shared a similar philosophy of ministry: we each believed it wasn't enough just to try to help others, we needed to empower them to be able to help themselves.

Eventually Conner woke up from his nap. When Brad brought him down to meet Sister Helen, we quickly forged another bond—she was instantly charmed by my son. What mother wouldn't appreciate that?

When it came time for Sister Helen to leave, she told me, "You don't know how nice this has been. How much meeting you has meant to me."

I told her I felt the same way about meeting her; that I hoped we could meet again. She assured me she would like that very much.

Before she left, she also said, "I really think you ought to consider writing a book of your own, Debbie." Other people had said that over the years, but it somehow meant more coming from her.

Even before I'd met Helen Prejean, when I'd heard people criticize her public position in the death penalty debate, I had respected her right to believe and act as she did. But now, having met her, I also respected her motives. And I respected her.

I had no doubt that she was doing what she felt God wanted her to do. And I hoped there would be opportunities for further developing our relationship in the future.

I was surprised and pleased when I received a phone call from Helen just a couple days later. She told me she was just finishing up the filming for a PBS "Frontline" documentary about the personal stories behind the movie *Dead Man Walking*. She assured me she hadn't used my name, but she'd told the director, Ben Loeterman, about meeting me, and how she'd been so affected by our conversation and impressed with my strength in the wake of all I'd been through over the years. "Ben said he'd really like to talk to you, but I told him I'd have to talk to you and ask if you wanted him to even know who you are."

"Who are these people?" I wanted to know. "What are they like?"

Helen gave me a little background. She obviously trusted them with her story. "If I had any doubts about them at all," she said, "I wouldn't have even called you."

I agreed to talk with them. "But no promises."

I'd been praying for months for an opportunity, any opportunity, to make something positive out of my negative past experiences. *Could this be it?* I'd been thinking more along the lines of volunteering at a rape crisis center or something like that.

I talked with *Frontline* producer/director Ben Loeterman and Chris Buchanan, his associate producer, a couple days later. Brad was out of town, so we met at his folks' house, where I could be more comfortable and his mom could babysit Conner in the backyard while we visited.

We talked for a couple of hours altogether. I summarized my experience and answered questions about everything from my attitude toward the death penalty to my feelings about Helen Prejean and her ministry. I could tell within the first few minutes, from the glances Ben and Chris were exchanging, that they wanted me to be part of their program. But it wasn't until the end of our conversation that they came right out and asked if I'd consent to an on-camera interview.

I told them I'd think about it; I'd have to talk the idea over with my husband before I gave them an answer. By this point, I felt strongly that this opportunity could be an answer to my prayers. I did want Brad's blessing, however, because going public like this was a big step. I needed to make sure Brad felt it wasn't right just for me, but that it was right for our family.

I would have to characterize his reaction as cautiously supportive. Brad hadn't been in on the entire conversation with Helen and he hadn't met the *Frontline* folks at all. While my positive feelings weren't enough to dispel his concerns, he'd been praying along with me as I'd asked God for some direction about what I might do. If I felt this was an answer, he was willing to go along, provided we proceed carefully, with our eyes wide open.

The *Frontline* people told me they wanted to get my reactions to the movie itself. Since I hadn't yet seen it, Brad and I took in a matinee showing late in the afternoon before I was to be interviewed that evening.

For me, the movie was emotionally excruciating. Sitting in a darkened theater for two hours watching someone who looked so much like Robert Willie seemed difficult enough. But what was even worse was having to also vicariously experience the emotions of so many characters in the movie. Not only did Susan Sarandon as Sister Helen Prejean and Sean Penn as the composite character named Matthew Poncelet make you feel their pain, but I found myself identifying with so many others: the parents of the murdered girl; Poncelet's brothers during their last visit with him just hours before his death; and especially the woman who played Sean Penn's mother, who wasn't even allowed to hug her son before he was led off to be executed.

Throughout the movie, I had to steel myself against what felt like a constant onslaught of psychic pain. I knew if I let down my defenses, if I let the full impact of the movie get to me, there was no way I was going to be able to regain enough composure to film the *Frontline* interview as scheduled that evening.

By the time the credits rolled at the end of the movie, I felt like an emotional basket case—on the inside. Outwardly, I hadn't dared allow myself to really react.

Brad's "protective husband" response to the movie didn't help my resolve. He was furious by the time we walked out of the theater. Not only was he reacting to Sean Penn's powerful portrayal of the man who'd kidnapped and raped his wife, Brad was angered by the way the movie attempted to make Matthew Poncelet a much more sympathetic character in the end by depicting obvious remorse.

We knew Matthew Poncelet was a composite character. We also knew, from Helen's book and from what she'd told me, that Patrick Sonnier, unlike Robert Willie, did have a real change of heart before he was executed. But Brad and I could only see Sean Penn as Robert

Willie. On the screen he *was* Robert Willie. So his sympathy-evoking display of remorse at the end seemed worse than dissatisfying; it felt somehow dishonest.

That made Brad indignant. While I had much the same reaction to the movie Brad did, I couldn't yet talk about it. I had an interview to do, and I had less than half an hour to compose myself enough to talk to a camera—not only about the most horrible experience of my life, but about the impact the movie had on me.

When asked about my reaction to the movie, the first thing I told Ben Loeterman, the director, was that the movie had really made me feel for Robert Willie's mother. Being a mother myself now, I could only imagine her pain. "I want to contact her," I told him. "I want to tell her I'm sorry and let her know that I'm okay."

That's when Ben told me Elizabeth Oalmann had died sometime earlier. It made me wish I'd tried to contact her when I'd forgiven her after Conner was born. Now it was too late.

Before we began the filming, I'd asked Ben what the interview would cover. He'd assured me, "Nothing we haven't already talked about." And he was right. It just took twice as long to get it all on film. I was nervous to begin with. Telling myself, *This may be my one chance to affect people with my story,* imposed a lot of extra pressure. By the time we wrapped up the session, it was almost midnight and I was emotionally wrung out.

Frontline needed two more scenes, which we shot over the next couple of days. First, they wanted film of me purchasing a movie ticket for a showing of *Dead Man Walking.* And then they wanted to shoot me talking with Helen Prejean.

We met Helen in a Catholic church over in New Orleans. As she and I sat on a pew and began talking, taking up our conversation and our new relationship where we'd left off at my condo a week or more before, the cameras began rolling. Before long, we were so completely engrossed in discussion we were oblivious to the cameras and production people milling around us.

Helen conducted a mini-Bible study, pointing out how people who favored the death penalty always sought biblical support in Old Testament passages about justice and punishment while pretty much ignoring the New Testament themes of redemption and forgiveness.

As Helen illustrated her point by thumbing from one passage to another in a dog-eared and heavily underlined Bible that had belonged to Patrick Sonnier while he was on Death Row, I was struck by the realization that I not only respected Sister Helen, I really liked her. We shared many of the same beliefs. As I listened to her speak so passionately about her convictions, I couldn't help thinking maybe God was using her to help me reconcile my long-term personal conflict between what I believed in my head and what I felt in my heart.

I saw and heard that conflict clearly and poignantly demonstrated in my own words the night *Frontline* aired the episode "Angel on Death Row." Sitting in front of the television set watching myself on network television was a strangely unsettling feeling. I was surprised at how much time I was given on this television documentary, which used the Academy Award-winning movie and the real-life stories (of Helen, Detective Mike Varnado, Robert Willie, Faith Hathaway and her parents, and me) as a thought-provoking case-study discussion of capital punishment. My own ambivalence was made clear throughout the program, but it was underscored and highlighted by the quote used to conclude the show.

Frontline had acknowledged that both sides in the death penalty debate liked to quote Scripture to support their opinions; that for years, both proponents and opponents of the death penalty had wanted me to join their causes; and that I was not nearly as concerned about which side was "right" as I was concerned about what God wanted and what he expected of me.

However, I admitted, and the program closed with this quote:

"If what I'm supposed to believe is that Robert Willie deserves his place in heaven right there next to me and Faith Hathaway and whoever else . . . then I'm not quite there yet."

Those words troubled me. Perhaps because they were my own.

I contrasted that statement with God's Word a couple months later when yet another Sunday school lesson practically jumped up and smacked me in the face. The Bible lesson that day came from Matthew 20:1–16, where Jesus begins a parable by saying, "The kingdom of heaven is like a landowner who went out early in the morning to hire men to work in his vineyard." He promised to reward them at the end of the day with a fair day's wage—one denarius. The laborers quickly agreed and worked hard all day. But the landowner, seeing how much work remained to be done, and noting how many unemployed people there were, kept adding to his work force throughout the day, promising each new crew that he would pay them fairly when they finished.

When evening came, the landowner ordered his foreman to pay the workers, starting with the last ones hired only an hour or so before. When each of the most recent hires received payment of one denarius, those who were hired first and who had worked all day expected to get more. When they also received one denarius, they began to grumble and complain.

But the landowner answered one of them, saying, "Friend, I am not being unfair to you. Didn't you agree to work for a denarius? Take your pay and go. I want to give the man who was hired last the same as I gave you. Don't I have the right to do what I want with my own money? Or are you envious because I am generous?"

I saw the application in those words even before our teacher went on to point out how God's idea of justice was so different from ours; how God's grace extended to any of us who were willing to accept it, no matter what we've done.

He made the point that as human beings we so often focus on justice that we fail to appreciate God's promise of grace. And if we want to insist on justice, we might do well to stop and realize, *God help us if any of us get what we deserve!*

Once again that day our discussion spoke directly to me. I recalled what I'd said on *Frontline* for all the world to hear and I thought, *Based on what Helen Prejean says, I don't think he did, but if Robert Willie truly repented and asked God's forgiveness before he died and is in heaven today, that is between him and God. It's not as if he could fool God into thinking he deserved to be there. None of us can.*

If he is there, as uncomfortable as I still am at that idea, I need to accept the fact that my human feelings won't really matter when I get to heaven. If Robert Willie is there, it'll be the same way I get there—only by God's generosity and grace.

Even as I thought this, I realized it's a hard truth to believe. The deeper the hurt, the harder God's standards of forgiveness and grace are to grasp, let alone embrace.

Shortly after that, Ben Loeterman called to tell me some sad news. Vernon Harvey, Faith Hathaway's stepfather, had died.

I talked to Helen later that same day. Helen said one of the Harvey's neighbors had phoned her. This woman had been so concerned about Elizabeth Harvey being alone, with no family or friends around, that the neighbor had wanted to call someone. Elizabeth evidently gave the woman two numbers: One belonged to Ben Loeterman of Frontline, who'd provided Vernon Harvey his last chance to speak publicly; the other was Helen Prejean's.

"I sent flowers. But I don't know what else to do, Debbie," Helen said. "Every attempt I've made to reach out to them in recent years has been rejected. My very existence seemed to cause them so much pain. I don't want to hurt Elizabeth any more. Not now, when she's already hurting so much."

I reported to Helen about my most recent contact with Elizabeth Harvey. She'd called just a week or two prior to the *Frontline* broadcast. It had been the first time I'd heard from her in years.

She phoned to say she'd learned from Ben Loeterman that I'd agreed to be interviewed for the PBS documentary. She told me she was glad to hear I was finally ready to speak out after all these years.

I didn't want to mislead her, so I said, "Mrs. Harvey, I don't think what I said on that program is what you want to hear."

"Well, it's important for people to hear from the perspective of the victims," she said. "Then maybe they'll understand the reason for the death penalty!"

I tried to choose my words as carefully as I could because I didn't want to upset her. "I don't see myself as a victim anymore," I told her. "I'm a survivor." It's a whole different mind-set. "And I'm no longer sure that the death penalty really accomplishes anything."

"HOW CAN YOU SAY THAT?" So much for not upsetting her. "You of all people. You know what Robert Willie did. You know how much he deserved to die!"

"I'm making no excuses for what he did," I tried to assure her. "There can be no excuse. And yes, I think he deserved to die. But what I'm saying is, the death penalty didn't do anything to heal me."

"Maybe you would feel differently if your child was murdered!" she told me.

"You might be right there," I admitted. "I'm a mother now, too. And I can't imagine what you must have gone through. How much you've been hurt. I'm so sorry about that, Mrs. Harvey. And my prayer for you and for Mr. Harvey is that you will some day be able to find God's peace."

But I didn't know if they ever would. My own experience had convinced me that God's peace can't be separated from his grace and forgiveness.

CHAPTER SEVENTEEN

Forgiving the Dead Man Walking

The public response to *Frontline's* "Angel on Death Row" episode shocked and nearly overwhelmed me. Newspapers from coast to coast noted my part in the story.

Hollywood's *Daily Variety* said,

"The documentary's scoop is an interview with one of Willie's victims, Debbie Morris of Madisonville, Louisiana, who has never before been publicly identified. Morris, who was abducted, brutalized, and raped by

Willie and his conspirator, managed to escape and inform police, leading them to her boyfriend, who had been shot, tied in the woods, and left for dead.

"Though Morris was never mentioned in the film or book, her testimony was essential to Willie's conviction. The focus of 'Angel on Death Row' is not, as the title would suggest, on the work of Prejean, but on the figure of Morris and her ambivalence over her role in Willie's execution.

".... 'Angel on Death Row' takes 'Dead Man Walking' one step further, both in time and ideology. Loeterman skillfully chronicles the ongoing recovery of Morris, and how her conscience has developed so that she might consider changing her views. In so doing, he successfully frames the death penalty debate, no mean feat considering its bewildering complexity."

The New York Daily News wrote,

"One survivor, at the time identified by the media only as 'a sixteen-year-old girl' speaks out on *Frontline* and identifies herself in a public forum for the first time. Her name is Debbie Morris, and whatever your view on the death penalty, she is all but guaranteed to both impress and surprise you."

But perhaps the most heartening review for me came from the *New Orleans Times-Picayune* the paper which had covered the original story so extensively years before:

"The surprise star witness is Morris, who was sixteen when Willie abducted her and her boyfriend in Madisonville. Her recollection of their nightmarish ordeal is chilling. But even more memorable is her description of the emotional and spiritual journey she's taken in the fifteen years since."

It has been a long, sometimes rocky road. But the journey continues.

When I agreed to do *Frontline* I'd thought it might be my one opportunity to finally speak out and make something positive out of all those years of negative experiences. Instead, that *Frontline* broadcast served as a critical turning point which, in turn, has opened up exciting new avenues I've only begun to explore—avenues that have already led me to new opportunities for sharing and personal growth.

My very first official invitation to speak about my experience came from the Metro Health Medical Center in Cleveland, Ohio. One of the chaplains there had seen me on *Frontline* and asked me to be a keynote speaker at a regional conference they were planning for hospital chaplains, pastors, social workers, counselors, and other caregivers. The conference, titled "Forgiveness in a Violent Society," was scheduled for the spring of 1997.

I wasn't sure what I had to say to such a group, but I agreed. And, as so often happens when I decide to do something to help others, I received far more from the experience than I gave.

The overwhelmingly positive response of the conferees to my story helped validate, in my own mind, the struggle and growth I've been through. Another one of the conference keynoters, former Beirut hostage Terry Anderson, shared the conference platform and encouraged me further by recommending I contact the agency that books all his speaking engagements.

The most meaningful benefit of all from that conference may have been the introduction Brad and I got to Dr. Terry Hargrave, a therapist and psychology professor from Amarillo, Texas. We formed an almost instant friendship with Terry, who not only added his voice to those encouraging me to get my story in print, but set up the contacts that led directly to the writing of this book.

But I'm most indebted to Terry Hargrave for the insights into my own experience and my own understanding of forgiveness I gained from sitting in on the seminars he led those two days in Cleveland. When he talked about the important "work of forgiveness" I thought, *It is work. I've learned that!* He divided the "work of forgiveness" into two areas or goals: salvage and restoration.

He pointed out there are times we've been hurt when the only reasonable goal is to find a way to get over the incident, to minimize the damage, to get on with the healing, to learn from the experience, and to move on. Making the best you can from a past experience is the goal of what he termed "salvage."

Restoration has a different goal. But the work of forgiveness can't achieve restoration unless there was a prior existing relationship or at least the desire for a relationship you want to restore.

I found this distinction between these two equally valid but very different goals of forgiveness—salvage and restoration—extremely helpful. For a long time, I made the mistake, like many people do, of thinking about forgiveness only in terms of the "restoration" model. I wondered if I really had forgiven Robert Willie, since I couldn't imagine ever wanting to interact with him or encounter him again—even in heaven. But Dr. Hargrave set my mind and heart at ease by saying that there are times when forgiveness won't, and shouldn't, result in restoration. There are cases, like my experience with Robert Willie, where there never was a relationship to be restored, when the highest goal we should seek is salvage.

Hargrave identified what he considered two "stations" that play an important role in this salvage process of forgiveness. The first is *insight,* where we recognize how we were violated and who has responsibility; this is critical in order to prevent the same thing from happening again. I needed insight to get past those feelings I had for so long that I was partially to blame for everything that happened to me because I'd been out too late the night of the kidnapping. Only with insight did I finally understand that Mark and I had been innocent victims; that the blame for what happened rested solely on Robert Willie and Joseph Vaccaro.

The second station that can play a part in the salvage process is *understanding.* Understanding is different from insight in that here you may be able to see *why* something was done. There's no attempt to deny or dismiss accountability, just a possible explanation as to how it happened. For example, I came to a better understanding of why Robert Willie's mother did what she did after I had a child of my own.

Insight and/or understanding allow us to salvage something from a hurtful experience. In that sense they can play a beneficial role in the work of forgiveness.

In Hargrave's model there are two additional stations in the restoration process of forgiveness. There's *overt forgiving,* where forgiveness is openly sought, given, and received. Apologies are made and accepted. Remorse is expressed and acknowledged. In my case, this was first forced in the therapy portion of my substance abuse treatment program. And it's happened more naturally in various situations since.

But overt forgiving isn't the only station through which restoration can be reached. Sometimes it occurs where there is an *opportunity for compensation.* My mom coming to help after Conner's birth was one example of this. She and I have had numerous other opportunities, before and since, when her loving actions have compensated for past hurts and helped us further along toward our goal of complete restoration in the work of forgiveness.

Terry's teaching helped put words to my feelings. He gave meaning to past experiences. He offered the beginnings of a solid framework I could use to organize and shape my own nebulous thoughts. I've had to spend a lot of time and energy doing just that as I've worked on this book and when I've had to respond to some of the tough questions my listeners always want to ask whenever I speak on my experience and forgiveness.

So many people ask me, "How can you forgive someone like Robert Willie?" They're incredulous at the very thought.

I understand the reaction—for a long time I felt the same way. But very recently I came across a wonderful book by Lewis Smedes titled *Forgive and Forget* (Pocket Books, 1986), which has helped crystallize my thoughts and express in more articulate words some of what my experience has taught me.

He has a section called "Forgiving Monsters" that seemed particularly relevant to my experience. Or to any of Robert Willie's victims. Or to anyone whose life has been impacted by some horrible wrong. Smedes writes, "If we say monsters are beyond forgiving, we give them a power they should never have. Monsters who are too evil to be forgiven get a stranglehold on their victims; they can sentence their victims to a lifetime of unhealed pain. If they are unforgivable monsters, they are given power to keep their evil alive in the hearts of those who suffered most."

I couldn't begin to articulate it at the time, but I understood that truth even before Robert Willie was executed. I knew I had to forgive him—not for his sake, but for mine. Until I did, there was no escaping the hold his evil had on my life.

People also ask me, "Is forgiveness really possible when a person doesn't ask for it? In a case like mine where a person who wronged me expressed no remorse? Or maybe in another case where a person doesn't even realize the hurt that was caused?"

Again, Terry Hargrave's teaching helped me here. He says we don't need a second person's involvement to experience the insight or understanding needed for the salvage dimension of forgiveness.

Lewis Smedes enlightened me further on this score when he wrote, "The climax of forgiveness takes two, I know. But you can have the reality of forgiveness without its climax. Forgiving is real, even if it stops at the healing of the forgiver."

What if I just can't forgive?" When people ask me that, what they often mean is, "What if I'm not yet ready or willing to forgive?"

Much, if not most, of the time our reluctance to forgive is based on the false assumption that forgiving means giving in or giving up something valuable. We think it might mean granting the other person some reward he or she doesn't deserve. Or completely discounting the wrong committed—as if it never happened.

But that's not how forgiveness works. By forgiving Robert Willie, I in no way absolved him of his responsibility for what he did to me, to Mark, to Faith Hathaway, or to anyone else. He has to answer for that. And he did. He can't pay any more than he has paid and is paying already. So forgiveness isn't giving him anything he doesn't deserve; he gains nothing from it.

However, the refusal to forgive him always meant that I held on to all my Robert Willie-related stuff—my pain, my shame, my self-pity. That's what I gave up in forgiving him. And it wasn't until I did, that real heal-ing could even begin.

I was the one who gained.

But sometimes forgiveness seems so hard! Is it really worth it?"

How badly do we want to be healed? For so many years my reluctance to forgive was like a darkness inside, a barrier that barred joy and love and so many good things from my life. Forgiveness smashed that bar-rier and has enabled me to experience the giving and the receiving of love again.

God's love. The unconditional love of a wonderful husband. The love of Conner and my new baby daugh-ter, Courtney.

My family relationships are being restored. I love and appreciate my mother more than ever today.

My dad has discovered the power of God's for-giveness in his own life. He's lived in the same home, been married to the same woman, and worked at the same job for over twenty years now. He's an active leader in his local church. This man on whom I blamed much of my family's instability has become for me an inspiring symbol of security and dependability through God's grace. He has slowly but surely worked at rebuild-ing his relationships with all of his children. And what a wonderful grandfather he is to my kids.

Forgiveness has made all that possible.

People often ask, "How do you feel about the death penalty now? Are you for or against it?"

I still have ambivalent feelings. I've seen mankind's idea of ultimate justice; I have more faith in God's. And even God seems to put a higher priority on forgiveness than on justice. We don't sing "Amazing Justice"; we sing "Amazing Grace."

Does that mean I think a holy God would oppose the execution of a convicted murderer like Robert Willie?

I don't know; I'm still wrestling with that question. But I do know this: Justice didn't do a thing to heal me. Forgiveness did.

We want to hear from you. Please send your comments about this book to us in care of the address below. Thank you.

ZondervanPublishingHouse
Grand Rapids, Michigan 49530
http://www.zondervan.com